FAKES AND FRAUDS

Previous Titles 1988–1996
IN THE
PUBLISHING PATHWAYS SERIES
ON THE
HISTORY OF THE BOOK

Edited by Robin Myers and Michael Harris

Pioneers in Bibliography. St Paul's Bibliographies, 1988

Fakes and Frauds. Varieties of Deception in Print and Manuscript. St Paul's Bibliographies, 1989

Spreading the Word. The Distribution Networks of Print 1550-1850. St Paul's Bibliographies, 1990

Property of a Gentleman. The Formation, Organisation and Dispersal of the Private Library 1620-1920. St Paul's Bibliographies, 1991

Censorship and the Control of Print in England and France 1600-1910. St Paul's Bibliographies, 1992

Serials and their Readers 1620-1914. St Paul's Bibliographies, 1993

A Millennium of the Book: Production, Design & Illustration in Manuscript and Print (900-1900). St Paul's Bibliographies, 1994

A Genius for Letters: Booksellers and Bookselling from the 16th to the 20th Century. St Paul's Bibliographies, 1995

Antiquarians, Book Collectors and the Circle of Learning. St Paul's Bibliographies, 1996

Fakes and Frauds

Varieties of Deception in Print and Manuscript

EDITED BY
ROBIN MYERS AND MICHAEL HARRIS

ST PAUL'S BIBLIOGRAPHIES
WINCHESTER
OAK KNOLL PRESS
DELAWARE

Reprinted 1996

First published 1989 by
St Paul's Bibliographies
West End House
1 Step Terrace
Winchester
Hampshire SO22 5BW

Published in North and South America by
Oak Knoll Press
414 Delaware St.
New Castle, DE 19720

ISBN 0-906795-77-X St Paul's
ISBN 1-884718-31-0 Oak Knoll

British Library Cataloging in Publication Data

Fakes and frauds: varieties of deception in print and manuscript.
1. England. Printing. Publishing. Printing & publishing. Forgery, history & fraud, history
I. Myers, Robin II. Harris, Michael, *1938–*
070.5'0942

ISBN 0-906795-77-X

Library of Congress Cataloging-in-Publication Data

Fakes and frauds : varieties of deception in print & manuscript / edited by Robin Myers and Michael Harris.
p. cm.
Originally published: Winchester, England : St Paul's Bibliographies, 1989.
Includes bibliographical references and index.
ISBN 1-884718-31-0 (hc)
1. Books—Forgeries—History. 2. Forgery of manuscripts—History.
3. Literary forgeries and mystifications—History. 4. Fictitious imprints—History. 5. Book industries and trade—History.
I. Myers, Robin. II. Harris, M. (Michael), 1938– .
Z1024.F25 1996
098'.3—dc20 96-43066
CIP

Cover illustration: "Fratres in Malo" from John Collier, *Human Passions Delineated* (Manchester: 1773)

Printed in the United States of America

Contents

Preface

FAKES AND FRAUDS was the subject of our tenth annual conference on aspects, sometimes rather peripheral, of book trade history, and the first under the auspices of the Centre for Extra-Mural Studies at Birkbeck College, University of London. It is our ninth publiction of the proceedings, and the second to be issued in hardback by St Paul's Bibliographies. The numbers of those attending have gradually grown over the decade, but this year they shot up from about 65 to more than 80 – partly owing, no doubt, to the intriguing title which attracted a general audience as well as book trade specialists. We hope that none was disappointed to find scholarship and entertainment combined in equal proportions as never before. On the one hand Lotte Hellinga and Michael Treadwell contributed their latest research on false and misleading imprints in the 15th and 17th centuries respectively while, in more light-hearted vein, Nicolas Barker and Tom Davis entertained us with the chicanery of recent literary forgery and criminally forged documents. There was also a wide timespan, from the 12th century, with Nigel Ramsay's paper on scriveners' seals, to the present day, and Michael Harris and Joseph Levine were at a mid point in both chronology and seriousness with new research, wittily presented, the one on the alternative trade and the other on forged editions of classical authors in the 18th century. In place of our customary workshop session we had a question-time during which pairs of speakers, with a chairman, took part in discussion and answered questions arising from their papers. This was both enjoyable and profitable but it was of the moment and did not seem to provide a basis for a written summary.

For November 1989 our theme will be the distribution of the printed word outside London. Our speakers will include Christine Ferdinand, Michael Harris, Ian Maxted, Robin Myers, Michael Perkin, Eiluned Rees and Tessa Watt and the subjects will range from the 16th century to the early 19th. John Feather will lead a discussion on pills and publishing in the 18th century provinces.

We are grateful to the British Academy whose grant to the tenth conference enabled us to invite two North American contributors.

Robin Myers and Michael Harris
London
February 1989

Contributors

NICOLAS BARKER is Head of the Select Materials Office at the British Library. He is Editor of the *Book Collector* and is a leading authority on printed forgery, from those of T.J. Wise to Mark Hofmann.

TOM DAVIS is a Lecturer in English at Birmingham University. He has specialised in the identification of 17th-century documents and works as a forensic handwriting consultant. He is currently engaged on a major study of European handwriting characteristics.

MICHAEL HARRIS is a Lecturer in History at the Centre for Extra-Mural Studies, Birkbeck College. He is Co-Editor of the conference papers and has written extensively on areas of newspaper history. He is General Editor of the *Journal of Newspaper and Periodical History*.

LOTTE HELLINGA is Deputy Keeper in Collection Development at the British Library. Her work on incunabula is internationally known.

JOSEPH LEVINE is Professor of History at Syracuse University, New York. He has written widely on the history of ideas, and is at present at work on a major study of the quarrel between the Ancients and Moderns. He is Paul Mellon Fellow at the Centre for Advanced Study of the Visual Arts (1988) and Guggenheim Fellow (1989).

NIGEL RAMSAY is a Research Editor on the *History of Canterbury Cathedral* and is attached to the University of Kent. He is interested in the medieval legal profession.

MICHAEL TREADWELL is Professor of English at Trent University, Ontario. He has published key studies of aspects of the 17th-century book trade as well as being a leading authority on the work of Jonathan Swift.

List of those attending the Conference

Jean Archibald
Librarian – Special Collections
Edinburgh University Library

Paul Baines
Junior Research Fellow
St John's College,
Oxford

T.A. Birrell
London

Eleanor Boulter
Librarian
London

R.K. Browne
Librarian
English Antiquarian Section
British Library

Gillis Burgess
Charity Officer
London

Richard Burleigh
Bookseller
Beaminster, Dorset

Jackie Canning
SCONUL Trainee
British Library

Leslie Carlyle
PhD Student
London

Tom Colverson
Retired Publisher/Lecturer
Oxford

Jan Conway
Reader Services Librarian
London College of Printing

Andrew S. Cook
Archivist
India Office Records,
British Library

Karen S. Cook
Map Specialist
British Library

Angela Craft
Book & Paper Conservator
London

Robert Cross
Book Publisher
Winchester

Nest Davies
Historical Research
Bradford on Avon, Wilts

John Feather
Professor of Library Studies
Loughborough University

William Fern
London

Keith R. Fletcher
Antiquarian Bookseller
London

Mirjam Foot
Librarian
British Library

Richard Ford
Antiquarian Bookseller
London

David Foxon
Oxford

Robin Francis
Librarian
National Art Library
London

B.A. Goldgar
Professor of English
Wisconsin, USA

Elizabeth Gray
Student
London

Stephen Green
Librarian
British Library

Anna Greening
Student – Nevadd Davies Bryan, U.C.W.
Dyfed

David J. Hall
Librarian
Cambridge University Library

Helen Hardy
Bookseller
London

Colston M. Hartley
Librarian
Surbiton

J.F. Hewish
Librarian
London

P.A. Hopkins
Historian
Cambridge

A.W. Huish
Retired Librarian
Essex

Arnold Hunt
Student
Trinity College, Cambridge

Elizabeth James
Librarian
British Library

M.J. Jannetta
Librarian
British Library

Graham Jefcoate
Librarian
British Library

Adrian D.S. Johns
Graduate Student
Cambridge University

Barry C. Johnson
Librarian
British Library

John Kinanne
Bookseller
Oxford

D.J.P. Laker
Banker
Surrey

Sheila Lambert
Cambridge

R.A.H. Lechmere
Bookseller
Worcester

C.L. Lee
Hertford

Elisabeth Leedham-Green
Assistant Keeper
Cambridge University Library

Anthony Lister
Retired Lecturer
Cheshire

James McGhee
Research Student
Glasgow

Dr Rosamond McGuiness
Lecturer
Royal Holloway & Bedford New College, London

Giles Mandelbrote
Research Student
St John's College, Oxford

Ian Maxted
Librarian
Exeter

John E.C. Palmer
Librarian
British Library

Charles Parry
Assistant Librarian
National Library of Wales

Margaret Payne
Librarian
Westerham, Kent

Michael Perkin
Retired Librarian
Wallasey, Wirral

Esther Potter
London

David W. Riley
Sub-Librarian
John Rylands University Library of Manchester

C. A. Rivington
London

H.M. Rosenberg
Lecturer
University of Surrey

Uta Schumacher-Voelker
Bibliographer
Oxford

Alison Shell
Research Student
St Hilda's College
Oxford

Mrs R. Shepherd
Manuscript Dealer
Surrey

Robert Sparks
Freelance Writer
London

Peter Stockham
Bookseller
London

Dr Katherine Swift
Shropshire

Peter Thorogood
Writer/Composer
West Sussex

A.T. Watts
Lecturer
Reading

Michael Winship
Research Student
Pembroke College Oxford

J.J. Wisdom
Librarian
Guildhall Library

P.K.J. Wright
Retired Librarian
Dyfed

Audio dictas dñoꝝ inimicicias ꝑ graciā dei cõsopitas q̄·
ꝓpter ⁊ spero ac ꝓpino de reliquo secundū maturiorē eta
tem me posse in ꝓprijs intendere corporis quieti animeqꝫ
saluti Hic itaqꝫ finis sit scripti. In nomine pris et filij et
spūs sancti Amen

Explicit itinerarius a terra anglie i ptes ierosolimitanas
et in vlteriores transmarinas editus pmo in lingua gallica
na a domino iohanne de mandeuille milite suo auctore.
Anno incarnacionis dñi M ccc lv. in ciuitate leodiensi ⁊
paulo post in eadē ciuitate trāslatus in dictā formā latinā
Quod opus vbi inceptū simul et cōpletū sit ipa elementa
seu singularū seorsū caracteres lrārum . quibus impressū
vides venetica/monstrant manifeste

Fig. 1 Printed in Venice?
Johannes Mandeville, *Itinerarium*
[Gouda, Gheraert Leeu, *c.*1483–4].
British Library, IA.47355, colophon.

'Less than the Whole Truth': False Statements in 15th-Century Colophons

LOTTE HELLINGA

ONE OF THE EARLIEST editions of the Latin text of John Mandeville's Travels ends with a colophon (fig. 1) that appears to be full of helpful information:

Explicit itinerarius a terra anglie in partes ierosolimitanas et in ulteriores transmarinas editus primo in lingua gallicana a domino johanne de mandeville milite suo auctore. Anno incarnacionis domini Mccclv. in civitate leodiensi et paulo post in eadem civitate translatus in dictam formam latinam. Quod opus ubi inceptum simul et completum sit ipsa elementa seu singularum seorsum caracteres litterarum. quibus impressum vides venetica monstrant manifeste.[1]

The beginning of the colophon is particularly specific about the origin of the text: 'the Itinerary of John Mandeville, from England to Jerusalem and lands beyond, first issued in the Walloon language, in the city of Liège, in the year 1355, and shortly after that date in the same city in a Latin version'. This statement is followed by an observation on the printed book that is actually in our hands: 'where this work was begun and completed, the elements, or characters of the single letters with which you can see it is printed, each show clearly that they are Venetian' – 'venetica monstrant manifeste'. A Venetian book, the reader would be justified in concluding, printed in Venice, and you would agree with the colophon that the textura typeface is in a style that you may call typical of countless Venetian books. It is true that early in its bibliographical history this Mandeville edition has briefly gone on record as a book printed in Venice, but in due course it was realized that this same printing type was used in many books printed in Gouda and in Antwerp by the printer Gheraert Leeu, his name clearly mentioned, and the Mandeville was confidently assigned to his press.[2]

It now became a bibliographical question whether the book was printed in Gouda or in Antwerp, which was most ingeniously settled by Henry Bradshaw who decided from features in the layout that the book ranged with books known to be produced in Gouda. But why that Venetian suggestion in the colophon?

We need to know a great deal more about the circumstances in which the book was printed before we understand that its colophon is half a boast, half a pun. In the first place, the chronological arrangement of Leeu's books of the period, and the

po[r] le corps & en sera plus seur & pl[us] en paix de
cõsciẽce. ¶ Le .x[e]. et derreniere obseruacion.
Item pour ceste cause, et pour ce que la
maladie corporele vient souuent pour
la maladie de lame. Le pape commande par
expresse decretale, a vng chescun medecin que
Il ne donne point medecine au malade, quãt
Il le visite, se non que parauant Il ait en-
horte de appeter le medecin de lame. Cest assa-
uoir son confesseur. Et seroit expedient en
chescun hospital, ou maison dieu que par or-
donnance faicte, on ne receupst aucun mala-
de qui ne se confessast des le premier Jour.
ou aumoins quil se representast au prestre
a ce ordonne. Comme Il est notablement
garde en lostel de dieu a paris.

¶ Explicit feliciter.

Aspice presentis scripture gracia que sit
Confer opus opere. spectetur codice codex
Respice q̃ munde. q̃ terse. q̃qz decore
Imprimit hec ciuis Brugẽsis Brito Johãnes
Inueniẽs artem nullo monstrãte mirãdam
Instrumẽta quoqz non minus laude stupẽda

Fig. 2. Printing invented in Bruges?
Jean Gerson, *Instruction et doctrine de tous chrétiens et chrétiennes*
[Bruges, Johannes Brito, *c.*1477].
Paris, Bibliothèque Nationale, Rés, D.7780, colophon.

pattern of the survival of copies, show us that the Mandeville was issued together with two other travellers' tales – the Ludolphus Suchen, *Iter ad Terram Sanctam*, and, more spectacularly, the editio princeps of the Latin version of Marco Polo's travels.[3] 'The Gouda Triplet', Henry Bradshaw called these three books, and the layout, with space for a very large initial capital in the Marco Polo, shows us that this was the book that had to come first in the volume. The Mandeville, the only one with a printer's colophon, was to come at the end. A Venetian pun at the end of a volume beginning with that most Venetian of texts makes some sense. But there is more. We now know that this typeface was not only Venetian in style, it was first used in Venice in a slighly different state, by the printer Reynaldus de Novimagio.[4] Gheraert Leeu used it in Gouda in 1483 (as well as a smaller Venetian typeface) after an interval in his production of over a year, during which we may reasonably assume (although there is no documentary evidence) that he visited Venice and brought home to Gouda, not only two typefaces of much higher quality and durability than anything he had used before, but also a Latin manuscript of Marco Polo. The printing of the travellers' tales in his brand-new type conveys a fine sense of elation after the widening of horizons, and the experience of a much greater world. 'Can't you see that this is a Venetian book?' the colophon asks, showing off the printer's trophies. Perhaps there is yet another dimension concealed here; Venetian textura was used for printing in Latin for the whole academic world until it was overtaken by Roman in the 16th century. In the 15th century, from *c.*1480 onwards, the printed book production of Venice itself was more significant in the academic world than that of all other centres of printing put together. A sample taken in England suggest that 58% of printed books used in Oxford and Cambridge in the 15th and early 16th centuries were printed in Venice alone.[5]

It is with this giant centre that Leeu began to compare himself in his outpost in Holland. Within a matter of months, however, he moved to Antwerp, at the time a modern centre of trade where he could successfully work for an international market: many of his books in Latin were sold to England, he also printed in English, and he had trading connections with France and Germany. The Venetian pun may therefore be taken as an exuberant declaration of intent to work in a world-wide dimension; although I do not think that Gheraert Leeu would have minded if his buyers thought that the book was really printed in Venice, his statement does not appear to be a serious attempt at deceit.

In another colophon (fig. 2) that I shall briefly discuss as an example of an obviously un-truthful statement, I see again more punning and perhaps self-mockery than intention to deceive. It is a colophon written by the printer Jean Briton, or Jan Brito, a scribe from Brittany who had settled in Bruges, and started printing about 1476. One of the few books known from his press ends with the declaration that he had printed this, 'while inventing himself the admirable art without instruction, nor [instruction] in the not less amazing instruments'. What does Brito claim here? Perhaps that he had not worked in somebody else's workshop to learn the new technique? Nobody except the odd local historian has ever believed that Brito had any serious claims to be the inventor of printing from the wording of this colophon, and it is generally left open to other interpretation.[6]

These two examples testify to the willingness of later readers to accept that a colophon may offer more than is superficially apparent, that a truth may be hidden there, but not quite in the way in which we expect to encounter it. But this tolerant attitude changes when a colophon appears to give us exact particulars about dates, printers and place of printing.

In such cases it is often forgotten that a colophon, a statement appended to a text giving particulars about its genesis or production, is a text in its own right, and is therefore open to interpretation according to the time, place and circumstances of its origin, as every text is. Interpretation is a function of context and situation – an *obiter dictum* that W. Hellinga's pupils used to be able to recite in their sleep. It may be worth repeating in the face of some of the problems presented by colophons.

A colophon is a statement, usually spoken in another voice than that of the author of the main text (or texts), and made at another time. And since this is a statement of facts that most bibliographers dearly want to know – the time and place of the production of the text in this particular material form – these facts are usually taken very seriously, and given almost legal status, as if they were a sworn truth. It is of course sound practice to assume that a text means what it says unless it can be proven to lie. Yet this denies the subtleties and delights that can be embedded in a text that flirts with the truth; or the revelations in those baffling, manifest un-truths in statements about time: how can it be that a printer is ten or fifteen years out in what appears otherwise to be a perfectly sober statement? How could such a slip of the careless hand go uncorrected? Slips and absent-mindedness serve as messages to reveal concealed inner mental states, as we all know in the wisdom of 20th-century psychology, but what kind of *Fehlleistung* makes the printer or compositor put the clock back to 1468 when the year is 1478, as in the first book printed in Oxford, or 1461, when the year is 1471, as with the famous *Decor puellarum* printed by Nicolas Jenson in Venice?[7]

What these strange slips, which both generated a bibliographical dispute and literature spanning more than two centuries, show beyond doubt, is our own preoccupation with time, our obsessive need to arrange these objects – printed books, as printed, in a sequence of time and place. They also show how difficult it is to grasp the import of a deviation of a literal truth, not only to catch nuances of sarcasm, irony, or deliberate playfulness, but to perceive what part of a statement is crucial to its structure, what is subordinate – where a compositor or printer could be allowed to lapse. In such subtle but profound changes in a colophon text, these curious mistakes resemble the questions posed by the presentation of illnesses as they change over the centuries, and are indeed close to such phenomena in so far as they are symptoms of changing mentality: the etiology of texts. Although germane to the theme of this conference of book-historians such an approach is generally remote from the way of thinking of the bibliographer. When a bibliographer encounters such errors or contradiction between statement and material evidence, he will tick the printer off, and may perhaps seek the historical context to explain the aberration. For not every manifestly wrong statement originates in the depths of the subconscious – there are instances where a reasonable ground for a misleading statement is obvious even to us. A.W. Pollard quoted in his *Essay on Colophons* a Politianus edition which states, quite simply, that it is printed in Florence in 1499.[8] In fact it is printed in types which belonged to Bernardinus Misinta in Brescia. Even so, Pollard writes, the fraud could have remained undetected, as it did for 400 years, if the book had not been mentioned in a petition to the Venetian Senate in 1502 where Aldus complained that a certain printer pretended that a book, protected by Venetian privilege, was printed in Florence whereas it was printed in Brescia. The fraud was a direct outcome of the first imperfect attempts to give the producers of books a reasonable copyright in them by means of privileges. As Brescia was subject to the Venetian Senate, Misinta could have been fined, had he put a truthful statement in his colophon, and he therefore used a false imprint and date to divert suspicion.

This colophon is by no means an isolated case. In a fascinating article on false information in colophons,[9] Curt Bühler quoted (from among a rich supply of examples) several cases of piracies, bogus Neapolitan or Sienese imprints produced in Venice and Milan, claiming to provide certain categories of books with a distinguished imprint, and mendacious colophons printed in Lyons, which purported to be Venetian or Bolognese. He also quoted over 30 examples of sheer carelessness and incompetence out of a number he called 'countless'. Bühler even gave examples of dates such as the 30th of February, the 33rd of March, the 31st of June, of numerous years long befor the invention of printing, and of unspeakable liberties with the Roman calendar.

Deliberate deceit can be brought about by competition, and also because of restrictions imposed by authorities. The more restrictions and interference, the more printers resorted to subterfuge; the introduction of control of the press and censorship in the 16th century offers rich material to illustrate the point. But we must also keep in mind what is, for us, an astonishing freedom with notions of time: time apparently was the vulnerable element in any statement concerning identity or leading to identification. Such weakness does not come to light until modern bibliographical methods detect conflicts between statements about time, and material evidence present in the book. Take, for example, the first book printed in Oxford with the printed date 1468, nine years earlier than any dated imprint in a book in England: its position in the hierarchy of the introduction of printing was hotly disputed, until it could be shown that the typeface did not exist, the paper was not made, until close to the date of 1478. It takes, however, a

.i. iste magister de babilone. In babilone enim or
tus est ubi et princeps gentis iudee extitit. et ac ult
Zoticus ca cum .i. uitalis Et corripit penul
Zozimus ma mum .i. uiuax uel uiuidus
Immensas omnipotenti deo pa
tri et filio et spiritui sancto gratiarum referimus acci
ones. qui nostrum catholicon ex multis et diuersis doc
torum texturis elaboratum atque contextum licet per mul
ta annorum curricula In M cc lxxxvj anno domini no
nis marcij ad finem usque perduxit Pro quo hoc so
lum mihi admodum necessarium. a uobis humiliter
deposco fratres et domini mei Inquantum peccatores fra
tres mei Inquantum iusti domini mei. quatenus pro me
peccatore philocalo ad deum preces porrigere uelitis
ut uestrarum precum interuentu. omnium meorum a deo
percepta uenia peccatorum. ad terram aptam ad terram
elisiam .i. extra lesionem positam. ad paradisi uidelicet
gaudia una uobiscum ualeam peruenire. ubi reg
nat examussim. dominus noster ihesus xpistus. dei filius
benedictus In cuius nomine flectetur omne genu
celestium. terrestrium. et infernorum. Cui est honor
et gloria magnitudo et magnificencia uirtus et po
testas regnum et imperium in secula seculorum Amen

Altissimi presidio cuius nutu infantium lingue fi
unt diserte. Qui que nimiosepe paruulis reuelat quod
sapientibus celat. Hic liber egregius. catholicon.
dominice incarnacionis annis M cccc lx Alma in ur
be maguntina nacionis incite germanice. Quam
dei clemencia tam alto ingenij lumine. dono que gra
tuito. ceteris terrarum nacionibus preferre. illustrare
que dignatus est Non calami. stili. aut penne suffra
gio. sed mira patronarum formarum que concordia propor
cione et modulo. impressus atque confectus est.
Hinc tibi sancte pater nato cum flamine sacro. Laus
et honor domino trino tribuatur et uno Ecclesie lau
de libro hoc catholice plaude Qui laudare piam
semper non linque mariam DEO. GRACIAS

Fig. 3. Date of printing ?
Johannes Balbus Januensis, *Catholicon*
Mainz [the Catholicon press, 1460, or 1469–70?].
British Library, C.14.e.1, colophon.

great deal of confidence in the comprehensiveness of our knowledge to arrive at any such certainty for anything produced in the past. For printing in the 15th century we are somewhat closer to that confident state than for most other periods of printing, but enough remains open to interpretation for discussions to continue.

The following discussion will illustrate this. It will concentrate on the colophon of the Mainz *Catholicon*, a famous book which has given rise to much controversy, especially in this century. Although few would deny that the colophon is striking, even moving, the words are open to many interpretations. The same can be said of the few facts which might lead to the identification of its printer and the circumstances of its production. It would take us too far in the present paper to discuss fully the various theories which have been built in the past and more recently around its production. In a study published in the *Gutenberg-Jahrbuch 1989* I present in the context of the assessment of bibliographical evidence an interpretation which leads to a new hypothesis about the dating and the production of the book. I submit this as a new alternative to other theories. The interpretation of the colophon which I present here forms part of my argument. This interpretation cannot be considered in isolation, without placing it in the context of data and circumstances of production. I shall therefore outline my arguments in brief, but refer for details and for supporting documentation and literature to the fuller discussion in the *Gutenberg-Jahrbuch*.

The Mainz *Catholicon* is a very substantial book, a dictionary compiled in the 13th century in Genoa by the Dominican Johannes Balbus, containing explanations of terms used in the Bible and preceded by a treatise on grammar.[10] It counts 373 leaves in royal folio format, and is printed in a small typeface, considerably smaller than any other type known to be used at the time. Its colophon (see fig. 3) contains a statement about the place where the book is printed, Mainz, and about the date, but the latter in an unusual form, using the plural 'annis' followed by roman figures for the year 1460. Nevertheless until recently the date 1460 has not caused much doubt. The *Catholicon* has therefore traditionally stood as a monument at the beginning of printing, after the Gutenberg Bible of 1455, the two Mainz Psalters of 1457 and 1459 and the Durandus *Rationale* of 1459. There has, however, been a long-standing division of opinion as to the identity of its printer. In 1460 only two printers' workshops were connected with Mainz – that of the inventor himself, Johann Gutenberg (but there is no documentary evidence of his whereabouts in 1460), and of Gutenberg's former associates Johann Fust and Peter Schoeffer, who had by then produced their two editions of the Psalter, the Durandus and in 1460 an edition of the Clementine *Constitutiones*, all signed with their names. The absence of a name was one of the arguments used in favour of Gutenberg, who never signed anything; on the other hand, many phrases in the *Catholicon* colophon are closely related to phrases used in colophons of Fust and Schoeffer. A third possibility, suggested early in this century, is that the book was printed by a partnership, a consortium of printers, but this suggestion, made by the great incunabulist Paul Schwenke, was neglected as the named printers found more favour as candidates. It is worth keeping this early suggestion in mind, though, in view of recent developments surrounding this question. Meanwhile, arguments and discussions raged until the end of the 1930s, without coming to a conclusion. At that time the discussion was usually referred to as the *Catholicon* controversy, and it is true that a certain amount of romantic sentiment and emotional heat attached to the questions surrounding this book.

The discussions about the *Catholicon* were revived with the development of the recording and dating of paper. It had long been known that all surviving copies of the *Catholicon* – and there are more than 70 recorded – are printed on three distinct paper stocks: there are copies of Bull's Head paper, on paper with an initial G called Galliziani paper, after its makers, and on a combination of two papers showing marks featuring a Tower and a Crown. There are only a very few leaves found in some copies which stray from this pattern, which was clearly established during the production of the book. There are also copies printed on vellum which have a few very minor variants in common with the Bull's Head copies. Otherwise all these states are printed from the same typesetting.

With the rapid development of the recording of paper in the 1960s it was first noticed by Dr Th. Gerardy that two of these paper supplies, the Galliziani and the Tower & Crown paper, certainly did not exist in the year 1460, but belonged to the late 1460s, and early 1470s. The Bull's Head paper, on the other hand, certainly existed in 1460, and was related to some of the paper known to be used by Gutenberg. Gerardy offered only very tentatively the hypothesis that all these books might have been printed in the late 1460s, some copies on an older paper stock, although, as he pointed out, paper was normally used soon after its manufacture. His suggestion was immediately dismissed by several historians of printing, but his findings were confirmed by technically more refined paper researches. These were the results of experiments in electron radiography conducted by Mrs Eva Ziesche and Dr Dierk Schnittger who then suggested three different datings for the printing of the three states of the book – 1460, 1469 and 1472. These three datings ignored the fact that the impression of type on the paper in each state is identical.

In a reaction to Ziesche-Schnittger, Dr Paul Needham confirmed their findings on somewhat extended material, and put forward an explanation to reconcile the three paper states with the identical impression: he agreed that printing did indeed take place at three different dates, not from movable type, however, but from 2-line units, solid pieces of metal cast as 'slugs', which were re-assembled on the two later occasions. This hypothesis was based on a number of observations which show that any corrections that were carried out in the type-metal affected the setting of two lines at a time, and that pairing of lines can sometimes be observed in other ways. Dr Needham concluded that the casting of text on solid line-pairs (or 'slugs') was Gutenberg's final invention. This view, with a touch of romanticism, had a wide appeal, and became known by the highly un-romantic name of 'the slug theory'.

I must admit that I found it difficult to accept this hypothesis, because I found that one observation, made over a large number of pages, consistently negates it: this is that when viewed on a collating machine, or by superimposing photographic negatives, a sharp image is obtained of large areas of the superimposed pages of any two different states. This indicates identical typesetting and it seemed out of the question to me that this material was re-assembled on two occasions. To obtain this sharp image one would have to posit that it was re-assembled with enormous precision using identical furniture, quoins, column dividers, etc. But I must add at once that the other evidence for the pairing of lines seemed to me to be correctly observed. Could there possibly be another explanation for line-pairs than the casting of slugs?

It appeared to me that there was a case for querying the evidence for the three widely separate dates of printing and I decided to re-assess the evidence, in the first place for the existence of the paper-stocks and also for the existence of the *Catholicon* itself between 1460 and 1470, and after 1470. This turned out to be a rewarding excercise.

For the paper-stocks I found that the paper-historians had dismissed without investigation a manuscript note of ownership and date on the final text-page in a copy (now in the Forschungsbibliothek in Gotha) of an undated German Bible printed at Strassburg by Heinrich Eggestein on Tower & Crown and on Galliziani papers.[11] The manuscript date in this inscription states that the book was owned by Steffan Losniczer Zum Stege in 1470 (see fig. 4). There seems no ground for doubting the truth of this statement, especially since a person of that name can be identified in Landshut in Lower Bavaria in the late 1470s.

Fig. 4. Not written in 1470?
Inscription on last page of text in the German Bible,
[Strassburg, Heinrich Eggestein, undated].
Gotha, Forschungsbibliothek, leaf 359 verso.

The date of ownership in 1470 shows that this large German Bible must have been in production by 1469; the dating 'not later than 1469' of the Tower & Crown paper therefore does away with any significant time-gap with the Galliziani paper of 1469. This has its consequences for the *Catholicon:* the conflict between colophon date and material evidence is hereby reduced to the question; the very year 1460 or the late 1460s?

In re-assessing the evidence for the existence of the book I found that there is considerable external evidence for the existence of the Mainz *Catholicon* from 1470 on: a copy in Basle University Library has a buyer's date in 1471 which is not ambiguous; the *Catholicon* is listed in 1470 in an advertisement for books issued by Peter Schoeffer in Mainz; there are several instances of printers' waste, especially of vellum strips printed on one side, used in bindings in Cologne in the early 1470s; and the book was used as *exemplar* for later editions from 1470 onwards. The book and its production clearly made an impact in a variety of ways. The pre-1469/70 evidence so far adduced is, on the other hand, all ambiguous or open to argument or interpretation. There is only one important piece of material evidence, a date of purchase purporting to be 1465, but this inscription is not beyond suspicion.

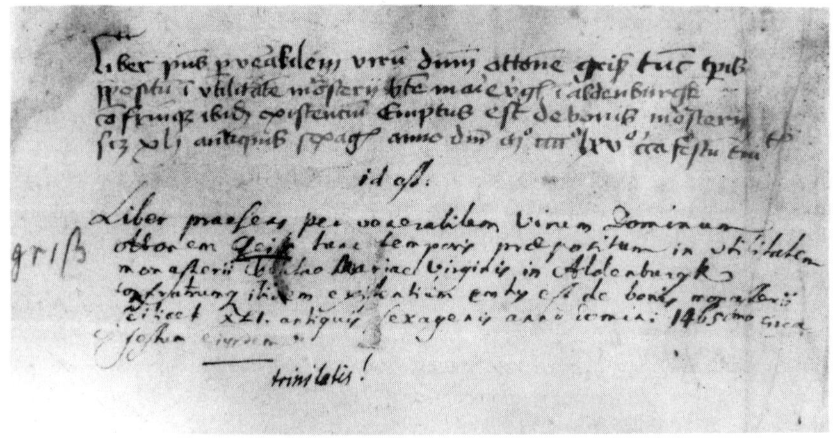

Fig. 5. Written in 1465?
Inscription in a copy of the Mainz *Catholicon* from the Bergerkloster, Altenburg.
Gotha, Forschungsbibliothek, flyleaf or original binding.

It is again a copy in the Forschungsbibliothek in Gotha, this time of the *Catholicon* itself, which was acquired in the 18th century for the ducal library at Gotha from the Bergerkloster in Altenburg in Saxony (see fig. 5). This copy bears on a fly-leaf in red ink the inscription which reads (with contractions expanded):

Liber presens per venerabilem virum dominum ottonem grisz tunc temporis prepositum in vtilitatem monasterij beate marie virginis in aldenburgk confraternitatis ibidem existentium Emptus est de bonis monasterij scilicet xlj antiquis sexagenis anno domini M° cccc° lxv° circa festum trinitatis.

There is still much to be uncovered about the history of the Bergerkloster, a house of the Augustinian Canons Regular, but it is known that in the 1470s a bitter dispute developed with the successor of Otto Grisz (the date of whose death is unknown), a prior named Pilgram von Ende. Pilgram apparently had contributed considerably to the financial disorder of the house and was forced to retire. Perhaps such a dispute may offer an explanation for the fact that the figures in the year date appear to be tampered with: the date 'lxv' is written in a different hand, possibly over an erasure. This variation in script makes the crucial date highly dubious as a witness for the existence of the book in the year 1465, and invalidates the sole piece of material evidence for the existence of the *Catholicon* by that time. All other arguments for a dating pre-1469 revolve round the wording of the colophon and its relation to other colophons.

We can therefore condense the argument even more. The 'slug-theory' is based on two assumptions: that all paper is always used shortly after its manufacture; and that we understand the wording of the colophon. The latter is what I want to discuss here, as an example of a complex situation underlying an enigmatic statement.

The *Catholicon* colophon with its printed date '1460' may appear to present an unambiguous statement (fig. 3). A.W. Pollard translated its text as follows in his *Essay on Colophons* (1905):

By the help of the Most High, at Whose will the tongues of infants become eloquent, and Who ofttimes reveals to the lowly that which He hides from the wise, this noble book, Catholicon, in the year of the Lord's Incarnation 1460, in the bounteous city of Mainz of the renowned German nation, which the clemency of God has deigned with so lofty a light of genius and free gift to prefer and render illustrious above all other nations of the earth, without help of reed, stilus, or pen, but by the wondrous agreement, proportion, and harmony of punches and types, has been printed and finished.
Hence to Thee, Holy Father, and to the Son, with the Sacred Spirit,
Praise and glory be rendered, the threefold Lord and One;
For the praise of the Church, O Catholic, applaud this book,
Who never ceasest to praise the devout Mary.
Thanks be to God.

In view of the ambiguity of the evidence for the existence of the book much before 1470 there is some cause to doubt the validity of the colophon date 1460. It is therefore possible to invoke precedent and point to the many cases where a colophon date in an early printed book, which on the face of it provides an equally unambiguous statement, could be proved to be a misprint.

In the case of the *Catholicon*, a misprint 1460 for 1470 was first suggested by Gerard Meerman in 1761, who a few years later revoked this idea when his attention was drawn to the Altenburg inscription with the date 1465; although he had not examined the inscription personally (nor had his informant Senator Duve of Hanover), he accepted its authority.

To assume a simple misprint '1460' for '1470' would make it possible to let the matter rest at this point. However, the text of the colophon is intriguing, and has aroused a great deal of discussion as to its meaning. It has always been read in isolation, in attempts to gauge whether these were words written by the inventor, or not, and if so, to interpret his statement about the nature of his invention.

Discussions in recent years on the validity of the date '1460' in the colophon have had very limited scope and concentrated on the term 'annis' in 'annis M cccc lx'. Although inconclusive, they point to an interpretation of the term 'annis' as a deliberate use of that unusual form.

The term was discussed by the late Professor Hans Widmann in the *Gutenberg-Jahrbuch 1973*; he cited a few instances in manuscripts where the plural seemed to indicate a particular (single) year. He concluded that if the colophon did not indicate '1460' it must be a matter of a misprint, not terminology.

In a further discussion in the *Gutenberg-Jarhrbuch 1975* Hildebrecht Hommel presented a more subtle reading of analogies in Latin, and concluded that 'annis M cccc lx' could well be read as an *ablativus respectus sive limitationis*, giving the meaning; 'in the years after 1460', 'in the years that end with 60' – which gives a rather sibylline tone which it is best not to ignore.

Widmann, however, proceeded in the same year to discuss the *Catholicon* colophon in particular in relation to the colophon of the *Vocabularius ex quo*, printed in Eltville in 1467 and 1469 which has several lines of verse in common with the *Catholicon* colophon. The texts of the *Catholicon* and the *Vocabularius* are related, although the *Vocabularius* is not a direct abstract of the *Catholicon*, as formerly thought. Both texts had an extensive dissemination in manuscript.

Widmann argued that the colophon of the *Vocabularius* (with three lines of verse) was ungrammatical, whereas the four lines of verse in the *Catholicon*, although not without grammatical defects, were at least coherent. He saw here proof that the *Catholicon* had preceded the first edition of the *Vocabularius ex quo* of 4 November 1467 and arrived at a dating for the Catholicon: 'not later than 4 November 1467'.

There is a weakness in Widmann's argument in that he did not consider the various other grammatical errors and inconsistencies in the colophons of the two works. He clearly measured the grammar according to standards which did not apply at the time for a text of this kind. Furthermore, with such an extensive and interrelated manuscript tradition of the two texts there seems no justification for regarding the two printed editions in isolation, and as exclusively dependent one on the other, as if there could be no influence from manuscript tradition.

The final four lines in the Catholicon colophon are printed on a new line and are therefore distinct. The two first lines of verse:

(1) Hinc tibi sancte pater nato cum flamine sacro
(2) Laus et honor domino trino et uno

have the familiar ring of countless scribal colophons, written in a style, sometimes half-humorous, that was to distinguish them radically from the preceding text. The scribe has the last word, as in (to take an arbitrary example) : 'Laudem do xp̄o,qui me liberavit ab isto'. There are countless examples, many in some kind of metre, and the lines in the *Catholicon* might be traced to any late-medieval manuscript as model. The two final lines, however, in the same metre, appear to be appropriate to ending the *Catholicon* text, because the reader (or perhaps the book, as my colleague Ronald Browne suggested) is addressed (or referred to) as 'Catholice:'

(3) Ecclesie laude libro hoc catholice plaude
(4) Qui laudare piam semper non linque mariam

Of the four lines of verse three are found in the two editions of the Eltville *Vocabularius ex quo* with dates in 1467 and 1469. It has been argued that these must have been copied from the *Catholicon*, with the obvious omission of the third line in which the word 'catholice' must allude to the *Catholicon* itself. If taken on their own this would indeed be a serious argument against a date of printing of the *Catholicon* later than 1467, in fact the only serious argument that remains for any date earlier than *c.*1469–1470. But I think one should take account of possible earlier models that the *Vocabularius* and the *Catholicon* could have had in common. In jingles of this kind so much can have happened: of an earlier example the third line, with different content, may have been omitted; the third line may have been re-coined for the *Catholicon* on the basis of an earlier model (for example: 'libro hoc *discipule*, or *presbitere*, plaude'); *anyone* could have written that line. The absence of this line of crooked verse in the first Eltville *Vocabularius* cannot stand as sole firm evidence for the existence of the *Catholicon* in 1467.

It therefore seems justified, *pace* Widmann, to consider the colophons in at least the wider context of the whole *Catholicon* colophon and its place among the *formulae* used in Mainz in printed colophons from the earliest in 1457 until 1472. For the sake of argument I propose to consider the *Catholicon* colophon, hypothetically, as undated, whether we base this on the precedent of wrongly dated editions, or on the interpretation of the term 'annis', and to investigate how it ranges within the chronological sequence of dated books with related colophons, almost all printed in Mainz.

In those colophons we can distinguish separate elements which are repeated in various combinations showing some major and minor variations. In the following list each of these elements is distinguished and indicated by a capital letter. The editions in which they are found are added in brackets. The list is limited to books printed before 1473, by which time everybody is convinced that the Mainz *Catholicon* existed in print. The core of these texts remained in use throughout the 1470s, especially in reprints, although new colophons tended to become increasingly voluble and complex.

LIST OF PHRASES DISTINGUISHED AS ELEMENTS

A (title), for example 'Presens clementis quinti opus constitucionum clarissimum'

B1 venustate capitalium decoratus Rubricationibusque sufficienter distinctus (1, 2, 3)

B2 Rubricationibusque sufficienter distinctus (4)

C1 Adinventione artificiosa imprimendi ac caracterizandi (1, 2)

C2 Artificiosa adinventione imprimendi ac caracterizandi (3, 4)

C3 Artificiosa adinventione imprimendi seu caracterizandi (5b)

C4 (sed) artificiosa quadam adinventione imprimendi seu caracterizandi (6a and b, 9, 10, 12, 14, 16, 20, 21, 22, 24)

C5 sed nova artificiosaque invencione quadam (11, 13)

D1 absque calami ulla exaracione (1)

D2 absque ulla calami exaracione (2, 4, 9, 10, 14, 20, 21, 22)

D3 absque calami exaratione (3, 5b, 18)

E sic effigiatus (1, 2, 3, 4, 5b, 6a and b, 9, 10, 12, 14, 16, 18, 20, 21, 22, 24)

F1 Et ad eusebiam dei industrie est consommatus (1, 3, 4, 5a and b, 6a and b, 9, 10, 11, 12, 13, 14, 16, 18, 20, 21, 22, 24)

F2 et ad laudem dei ac honorem sancti Jacobi (2)

G1 Alma in urbe maguntina. inclite nacionis germanice. quam dei clementia tam alti ingenii lumine. donoque gratuito ceteris terrarum nacionibus preferre. illustrareque dignatus est (6b, 9, 10, 12)

G2 ... tam alti ingenii lumine ... dignata (14, 20, 21, 22, 24)

G3 ... tam alto ingenii lumine ... dignata (16)

G4 ... tam alto ingenii lumine ... dignatus (Cath)

H Non atramento. plumali canna neque aera (6a and b, 7, 8, 12, 16, 23, 24)

I Sed arte quadam perpulcra. manu Petri [de gernsheim] pueri mei feliciter effeci finitum (7, 8)

K Non [calami] stili aut penne suffragio (11, 13, Cath)

L [Sed mira] patronarum formarum que concordia proporcione [et modulo]. impressus [atque confectus est] (Cath, abbreviated in 15)

M Hinc tibi sancte [pater] nato cum flamine sacro. Laus et honor domino trino tribuatur et uno. Qui laudare piam semper non linque mariam (11, 13, Cath)

N Ecclesie laude libro hoc catholice plaude (Cath)

O Altissimo presidio cuius nutu infantium lingue fiunt diserte. Qui que numerosepe parvulis revelat quod sapientibus celat (Cath)

P Name of printer(s) (1, 2, 3, 4, 5, 6, 9, 10, 11, 12, 13, 14, 16, 18, 20, 21, 22, 23, 24)

Q Date Q1: Anno dñi (1, 2, 3, 4, 5b, 6, 11, 13, 14, 16, 21, 22)

Q2: Anno dñice incarnacionis (5a, 10, 12, Cath, 18, 20, 23, 24)

Q3: Anno (7, 8)

LIST OF EDITIONS WITH RELATED COLOPHONS PRINTED BEFORE 1473 (ALL EXCEPT THREE PRINTED AT MAINZ)

1. *Psalterium*, 14 August 1457
2. *Psalterium*, 29 August 1459
3. Duranti, *Rationale*, 6 October 1459
4. Clemens V, *Constitutiones*, 25 June 1460
5. *Biblia Latina*, 14 August 1462 (5a: short, 5b: expanded colophon)
6. Bonifacius VIII, *Liber VI Decretalium*, 17 December 1465 (6a: short, 6b: expanded)
7. Cicero, *De Officiis*, 1465
8. Cicero, *De Officiis*, 4 February 1466
9. Thomas Aquinas, *Summa Theologica, Secunda pars Secunde*, 6 March 1467
10. Clemens V, *Constitutiones*, 8 October 1467
11. ELTVILLE: *Vocabularius ex quo*, 4 November 1467
12. Justinianus, *Institutiones*, 24 May 1468
13. ELTVILLE: *Vocabularius ex quo*, 5 June 1469
14. Thomas Aquinas, *Super quarto libro Sententiarum*, 13 June 1469
15. NUREMBERG: Franciscus Retza, *Comestorium vitiorum*, 1470
16. Bonifacius VIII, *Liber VI Decretalium*, 17 April 1470
17. Hieronymus, *Epistolae*, 7 September 1470

18. Mammotrectus, 10 November 1470
19. Valerius Maximus, 14 June 1471
20. Clemens V, *Constitutiones*, 13 August 1471
21. Thomas Aquinas, *Summa Theologica, Prima pars Secunde*, 8 November 1471
22. *Biblia Latina*, 23 February 1472
23. Gratianus, 13 August 1472
24. Justinianus, *Institutiones*, 29 October 1472

The use of these elements and their distribution over the editions can be summarized in the following diagram (fig. 6.).

			(A)	B1	B2	C1	C2	C3	C4	C5	D1	D2	D3	E	F1	F2	G1	G2	G3	G4	H	I	K	L	M	N	O	(P)	Q1	Q2	Q3
1. 1457, 14.VIII	Psalterium		A	B1		C1					D1			E	F1													P	Q1		
2. 1459, 29.VIII	Psalterium		A	B1		C1						D2		E		F2												P	Q1		
3. 1459, 6.X	Duranti		A	B1			C2						D3	E	F1	F2												P	Q1		
4. 1460, 25.VI	Clemens V		A		B2		C2					D2		E	F1													P	Q1		
5. 1462, 14.VIII	Biblia Latina	a	(A)												F1													P		Q2	
		b	(A)					C3					D3	E	F1													P	Q1		
6. 1465, 17.XII	Bonifacius	a	A						C4					E	F1						H							P	Q1		
		b	A						C4					E	F1		G1				H							P	Q1		
7. 1465	Cicero		A																		H	I						(P)			Q3
8. 1466, 4.II	Cicero		A																		H	I						(P)			Q3
9. 1467, 6.III	Thomas Aquinas		A						C4			D2		E	F1		G1											P	Q1		
10. 1467, 8.X	Clemens V		A						C4			D2		E	F1		G1											P		Q2	
11. 1467, 4.XI	ELTVILLE, Vocabularius		A							C5					F1								K		M			P	Q1		
12. 1468, 24.V	Justinianus		A						C4					E	F1		G1				H							P		Q2	
13. 1469, 5.VI	ELTVILLE, Vocubularius		A							C5					F1								K		M			P	Q1		
14. 1469, 13.VI	Thomas Aquinas		A						C4			D2		E	F1			G2										P	Q1		
date?	Catholicon		A																	G4			K	L	M	N	O			Q2	
15. 1470	NUREMBERG, Fr. Retza																							L							
16. 1470, 17. IV	Bonifacius VIII		A						C4					E	F1				G3		H							P	Q1		
17. 1470, 7. IX	Hieronymus		A	(independent)																								P	Q1		
18. 1470, 10.XI	Mammotrectus		A						C (var)				D3	E	F1													P		Q2	
19. 1471, 14.VI	Valerius Maximus			(independent)																								P			Q3
20. 1471, 13.VIII	Clemens V		A						C4			D2		E	F1			G2										P		Q2	
21. 1471, 8.XI	Thomas Aquinas		A						C4			D2		E	F1			G2										P	Q1		
22. 1472, 23.II	Biblia Latina		(A)						C4			D2		E	F1			G2										P	Q1		
23. 1472, 13.VIII	Gratianus		A	(independent)														G2 (var)			H							P		Q2	
24. 1472, 29.X	Justinianus		A						C4					E	F1			G2			H							P		Q2	

Fig. 6 Distribution of colophon elements over editions.

The colophons all praise the great invention, and appear in each instance to be a short ritual, first conducted in the printing house and thereafter, forever, between printer and reader, lest we forget the greatness of the technical miracle by which the book was produced. It is a reminder that praise is due to God for this invention, as well as gratitude that he granted the city of Mainz a privilege above all others. It is a formal celebration of completion, in its consistency over many years unparallelled in colophons printed elsewhere. It is also ritualistic in the sense that the same or similar words and phrases were repeated over and over again. In the diagram it can be seen how the phrases evolved, sometimes to reach a stable form, e.g. C4 'sed artificiosa quadam adinventione imprimendi seu caracterizandi' which was used eleven times, after three earlier versions. Some elements were replaced by new elements: H 'Non atramento plumali canna neque aera' is introduced as an alternative to D 'absque calami (ulla) exaracione'. The two never appear together.

If, for the sake of the argument, we exclude the *Catholicon*, there emerges an obvious development in both length and imaginative form of expression. The first four colophons (1457–1460) are short, each consisting of five elements plus title, date and name of printers. Then follow two instances of colophons existing in both a short and a longer form. In the 1462 Bible this is merely the addition 'artificiosa adinventione imprimendi seu caracterizandi'. In the 1465 Bonifacius there is in the second version a much longer and more important addition: 'Alma in urbe maguncie ... dignatus est'. In both versions of this colophon the longer element H (quoted above) is introduced. In the two Cicero editions the awareness of the non-Christian status of the text is seen in the use of plain 'Anno' in the date, against the 'Anno domini' or 'Anno dominice incarnacionis' of the other colophons. The new art is mentioned, however. After the death of Fust in 1466 the two substantial books printed in 1467 have much in common with the 1465 Bonifacius, but we find the shorter formulation D instead of H. In 1468 the Justinian conforms exactly to the Boniface of 1465, but included at the end of this book we find also the famous twelve lines of obscure verse on the invention of printing which were reprinted in the edition of 1472. At that time someone in Mainz must have delighted in producing difficult, punning and allusive Latin verse, compact with meaning which is (at least partially) bound to elude us. It has often been thought that the author of the verse in the Justinian may be the same as the author of the *Grammatica Rhythmica* of 1466 (a revised edition in two parts, *c.*1470 and 1473), usually referred to as Johannes Brunner, although we cannot be sure about his name, and of whose identity we know nothing, but of whom there is good reason to assume that he had close connections with Schoeffer's workshop. The edition of Jerome's *Epistolae* of 1470, which also contains verse at the end, is the first great edition with a long and independent phrasing of the praise of printing and of Mainz, as can also be found in the Valerius Maximus of 1471 and in the Gratian of 1472. Meanwhile, seven major books printed between 1469 and 1472 had the earlier phrasing.

The wording in the colophon of the Thomas Aquinas of 13 June 1469 follows exactly that used in the Aquinas edition printed two years earlier, and the Boniface of 1470 similarly reprints the longer colophon of 1465. The Mammotrectus of 10 November 1470 has a relatively curt reiteration of the pre-1465 formulae; the Clemens V of 13 August 1471 reprints the colophon of the same text completed in 1467, the Thomas Aquinas *Summa*, Prima Secunde, of 8 November 1471 reprints the colophons of 1467 and 1469, but the Latin Bible of 1472, by adding element G, presents a more elaborate colophon than the longest of the two variants printed in 1462.

There is, however, a small grammatical variation in several of these editions. The long passage in praise of printing in Mainz, passage G, beginning with 'Alma in urbe maguntie', is first found in a dated edition in 1465. Two corrections were introduced into its dubious grammar, one in 1469 and one in 1470. Both apparently aimed at improving the grammar with a minimum of change. One is the form 'dignatus', which had either no subject, or was mis-matched with 'Maguntia', which was the city graced above all others. In the Thomas Aquinas of 1469 we find the more logical and correct form 'dignata'. The other is in the words 'alti ingenii lumine', where in 1470 the word 'alti' is changed into 'alto', with some improvement of meaning.

1465	Boniface	G1	alti		dignatus	
1467	Thomas Aquinas	G1	alti		dignatus	
1467	Clemens V	G1	alti		dignatus	
1468	Justinianus	G1	alti		dignatus	
1469	Thomas Aquinas	G2	alti			dignata
1470	Bonifacius VIII	G3		alto		dignata
1471	Clemens V	G2	alti			dignata
1471	Thomas Aquinas	G2	alti			dignata
1472	Biblia latina	G2	alti			dignata
1472	Justinianus	G2	alti			dignata
?	Catholicon	G4		alto	dignatus	

From this survey it will be evident that the variations in this passage do not offer a base for a finely drawn *terminus ante*, or *post*, *quem*. But it is evident that the tinkering with the grammatical inflexions, the awareness of meaning expressed in subtle changes, belong to the years 1469 and 1470.

This period fits in with the increased freedom and signs of inventiveness which we can see beginning in 1465 with the second colophon to the Boniface, but which grow visibly with the verse in the 1468 Justinian and 1470 Jerome. The obscure and poetic allusions to printing in the *Grammatica Rhythmica* of 1466 may well also be relevant in this context. Almost entirely independent phrasing begins to appear in 1470 (Jerome) and 1471 (Valerius Maximus). In the full sequence of Mainz colophons, which are all (except the *Catholicon*) known to have been produced in the Fust & Schoeffer and Schoeffer printing house, the freedom and inventiveness of the *Catholicon* colophon does not fit in easily with the highly formalized colophons known to belong to 1457–1462; it is much closer to the colophons published from 1465 on, and in particular in the years 1468–1470 when we see improvement of grammar as well as the introduction of a distinct style:

punning and enigmatic, enigmatic also in the sense that it challenges the reader to unravel its elegant intricacies. It may not be too fanciful to imagine that someone in Mainz had become interested in printing and delighted in finding new formulae for praising the new art.

The punning obscurity of the *Catholicon* colophon lies in the lines that are peculiar to this colophon alone: the opening clause which introduces the date and place of printing, the lines about the 'mira patronarum formarum que concordia proporcione et modulo', an abbreviated version of which was taken over in a Nuremberg colophon in 1470, and the closing lines, one of which appears to be particularly apposite to the text. Let us first take up the challenge of the opening lines:

> Altissimi presidio cuius nutu infantium lingue fiunt diserte. Que que numerosepe parvulis revelat quod sapientibus celat. Hic liber egregius. catholicon. dominice incarnacionis annis M cccc lx Alma in urbe maguntina (etc.) . . .

The first two words are a devout but also rhetorically effective beginning, followed by two quotations from the Scriptures which deflect the high-flowing tone to a tender humility. We find here the traditional juxtaposition of the two Testaments, following Augustine's word that 'Novum Testamentum in Vetere latet, Vetus in Novo patet'. The first quotation, 'Quoniam sapientia aperuit os mutorum et linguas infantium fecit disertas' is from the Old Testament (*Wisdom* 10:21); the second a paraphrase of a parallel text in the Gospels of St Matthew and St Luke: 'In illo tempore respondens Iesus dixit: Confiteor tibi Pater Domine caeli et terra, quia abscondisti haec a sapientibus et prudentibus et revelasti ea parvulis' (*Matthew* 11:25, *cf. Luke* 10:21). The careful balance of the two Testaments suggests that these words are to be taken seriously. These texts, with their depreciation of the wise and learned in favour of the young and simple, are on one level of interpretation appropriate to the learned lexicon that they conclude: it is the *sapientes* who need this learned book in order to understand the Bible text, the meaning of which is revealed by the gift of God to the *parvuli* without such intervention. It is obvious to relate the opening lines to the production of the book, for giving such information is the function of a colophon. The lines have even been read as a formulation of modesty on the part of the inventor of printing, and taken as an argument that Johannes Gutenberg was the printer of the book, for who else could disclaim with such humility the personal merits of the invention? It is doubtful, however, that such sentiments were commendable much before the 19th century; they certainly do not appear to me to belong to the moral values of the fifteenth.

It appears to be more in accordance with late-medieval stylistic forms to put the emphasis on the *concealment* that is expressed here: something is concealed to the wise and sophisticated – namely the wise who have just finished consulting this enormous and learned book. The text is not only enigmatic, it can be read as an enigma – a classical and post-classical form that was still alive at that time. Playing with enigmatic forms of language certainly flourished in the Mainz workshop of Peter Schoeffer, as witnessed by the *Grammatica Rhythmica* and the lines of verse in the Justinian editions and the Letters of Jerome. A classic enigma is a play on the unexpected and the obvious; obvious to the initiated, but the outsider will never know the answer unless, revealed by intuition or divine inspiration, he sees things as they are and not as they seem to be.

In the Catholicon colophon the text leads us explicitly to concealment ('celat'). Since these lines introduce statements about the date and place of printing and the wonders of the printing process we may be justified in thinking that that is where concealment lies. In relation to the book the *sapientes* would be its readers, but the *parvuli* are less clear; are they the unsophisticated, the 'simple persons' in the term William Caxton would use to refer to himself and his role in the transmission of a text, not many years later? Perhaps we may even find, on a mundane level, an uncomplicated answer: the *sapientes* for whom the book is printed are not initiated in the process of printing and all that is behind it. But there are *parvuli*, simple persons, to whom the contents of the learned dictionary are a closed book, but who know all about the glorious invention and how to apply it.

I suggest we should explore the possibility of seeing the opening of the colophon as a formula for posing a riddle (and we have to imagine the dead-pan face, the twinkle in the eye and the raised finger which all belong to the ritual, and the iconography, of the presentation of a riddle). The text challenges us to ask: what can be concealed here, what is it we do not see? Or perhaps, think we see while we do not see? How are we hoodwinked?

We can work by elimination: the challenge to the enigma is followed at once by a statement of the text 'Hic liber egregius catholicon': the identity of the book cannot be in question. Then we have a statement of the date 'annis 1460' of which we have already discussed the problems posed by the term 'annis,' an unusual term, and if it is indeed an *ablativus limitationis*, as suggested by Dr Hommel, certainly something of a teaser. The elaborate statement of the place of printing again leaves no doubt. But two things strike us as unusual when we compare this sequence with other colophons produced in Mainz. What is conspicuously missing here is the name of a printer or printers; and secondly, the position of the date is in conflict with all the other Mainz colophons until the Gratianus of 1472, and indeed with the conventions of colophon statements: the usual form, which is represented in the 18 colophons printed until 1472 is to present the name of printer(s) and date in conclusion. In colophons printed in Mainz from 1473 on a second tradition begins, in which the colophon opens with a statement of date and ends with the name of the printer, in this case always Peter Schoeffer. Its unusual position, as well as the fact that it follows the introduction to an enigma is a reason, additional to the unusual form 'annis', to suspect that there is more to this date than immediately meets the eye.

There is, as we all know, Mainz printing where the name of the printer (and indeed a colophon) are notoriously absent: everything printed by Johann Gutenberg. The absence of a name has been a long-standing argument in favour of considering Gutenberg the printer of the *Catholicon*. Here all depends on what value can be attached to the other evidence for its dating which I have partly sketched. If we pursue the alternative theory, which assumes that the book was printed without intervals between states at the time of the two later paper-supplies, i.e. *c.*1469, it would have been produced after Gutenberg's death in 1468. We could then reason that the absence of a printer's name would mean that it was *not* printed by the firm of Peter Schoeffer, and it would be possible to propose as a reasonable alternative that the book was commissioned by the owner of Gutenberg's materials, Dr Conrad Humery.

There is one important document that enlightens us about the status of Gutenberg's possessions and about Dr Humery. It is a letter to the Archbishop of Mainz, Adolph von Nassau, written shortly after Gutenberg's death in February 1468, by Dr Humery in Mainz in which he confirms that he was granted by the Archbishop the full possession of everything left in Gutenberg's printing shop. Humery had owned these materials from the early 1460s as security for a loan, while the usufruct remained with Gutenberg. But there was one important condition of a restrictive and protective nature imposed by the Archbishop: the materials had to be used in Mainz only, and were not to be sold outside Mainz.

This circumstance – materials left after Gutenberg's death – would go a long way towards explaining how, exceptionally, a supply of paper and type which were both several years old, came to be used. We can then think again of the consortium of printers, as originally proposed by Schwenke. In this case the colophon would be silent about the circumstances of the production of the book which are concealed rather than merely unstated; the colophon would hide the name or names of those who were behind the production of the book, while proclaiming itself emphatically as a book produced in Mainz.

Scrutiny of the text of the colophon can lead to speculation. This is therefore a good point to recap the various kinds of evidence with which we are dealing. Material evidence in the form of the three distinct paper stocks points to a conflict in dating between the traditional reading of the colophon and the actual time of its production. External and circumstantial evidence leads to a date of printing in the late 1460s. A revised reading of the *Catholicon* colophon, in which we can distinguish several layers – Mainz formulae, earlier manuscript formulae and *ad hoc* phrases – would allow for such an interpretation. But a new hypothesis needs a widening of the material evidence on a basis of further observation to explain more fully the circumstances of the production of this book. And finally we need to broaden the historical context for a fuller understanding of such circumstances.

In the last few years the book has been examined on a scale as never before. Stimulated by Dr Needham's bold hypothesis, Dr Martin Boghardt has travelled the world and examined all 70 surviving copies with particular attention to correction by means of the cancellation of leaves, which confirmed that correction took place two lines at a time; the great care taken with correction is a general indication of overriding concern for producing a correct text. Dr Needham himself examined many more copies in addition to those that had formed the basis for his first publication. Blind impressions, damage to the impressions on the page, were examined and interpreted on both sides of the Atlantic. In December 1985 a conference was held at the Herzog August Bibliothek in Wolfenbüttel, on the initiative of Dr Boghardt, devoted entirely to the questions of the *Catholicon.* Gradually, but only very gradually, the book appeared to give up some of its secrets. I have to resort again to drastic summarizing, to end with a speculative last interpretation of the colophon, and refer again for all supporting material evidence and documentation to the full treatment in the *Gutenberg-Jahrbuch 1989*.

In extensive observations shared with friends with greater specialist knowledge and experience of typography than I have – Walter Partridge, Nicolas Barker and James Mosley– we arrived at the conclusion that the book was produced with three different lock-ups of the same typesetting, at three different presses, reflected by the three paper stocks. It was printed in movable type. The two-line effect was not caused by solid two-line blocks of types. This established, a further hypothesis emerged. Blind impressions of quads visible in substantial parts of the book, and occasional blind impressions of what appears to be wire, or the ends of pieces of wire, led to the surprising suggestion made by James Mosley that the type was secured with wire two lines at a time; a time-consuming process that cannot have been often repeated in the history of printing. A few allusions to such a process have filtered down in history, but it seems unlikely that many books have been produced in this way.

Why should anyone have chosen such a cumbersome procedure to produce a book? When trying to find an answer we have to go beyond the interpretation of observations and other evidence, and speculate on a historical context.

Whether (according to Dr Needham's hypothesis) printed at intervals of time from reassembled slugs, or (according to mine) divided between presses working in collaboration, the printing of the *Catholicon* resulted in an unusual book, an experiment in the new art of printing books. In the second hypothesis there is no major technical innovation, although there is a variation from what we think are ordinary procedures of the time; but, more important, an innovation in organization and in division of labour. Behind this may also lie a sharing of responsibilities of two kinds: for the accuracy of the text and financial responsibility. What we perceive may well be a redeployment of investment. We may speculate whether such an innovation took place in response to particular circumstances, and I have already connected this with the materials left by Gutenberg and from 1468 on in the possession of Dr Conrad Humery. Humery, born around 1400, and Doctor in Canon Law, had long been a very prominent citizen who attained the position of Syndic and Chancellor of the City of Mainz. He was also clearly a man of letters and had translated Boethius into German. He had taken an active part in the dreadful Mainz War in 1461–63, in which he had been the most influential supporter of Archbishop Dietrich von Isenburg. It is probable that he was banished from Mainz when Dietrich's opponent, Adolph von Nassau, won the city in 1462. In the autumn of 1463, when peace was made, Dr Humery was reinstated and compensated at Dietrich's request. Humery was a rich man, and had provided loans to other citizens of Mainz on several occasions. On the basis of his declaration to his former oppressor Archbisop Adolph von Nassau of 1468 it is thought that he lent Gutenberg money after the conclusion of the inventor's agreement with Fust, and that he held Gutenberg's typographical assets as collateral security. Thus, after the death of the inventor, he may have wished, at last, to realize the assets that until then had only nominally been in his possession, and, perhaps because they had been unused for a long time, to waste no time doing so.

It is at this point, in seeking a set of circumstances that would have allowed materials (paper and type) to lie unused for a number of years, that we have to speculate that at the time of the Mainz War (1461–63), and in his declining years plagued by old age, shortage of funds and, through changed circumstances, uncertain patronage, Gutenberg was not capable of carrying out plans he may still have cherished, and of making use of materials that were still available to him, although morgaged to his creditor. In 1468 Humery was himself in his late sixties and approaching the end of his life (he died probably in 1472), but not too old to commission the printing of a book. His choice was a reference work for which demand was certain, a guide to the reading of the Latin Vulgate Bible, the printing of which had been the glory of Mainz and Gutenberg. Perhaps it was the book that Gutenberg had always planned to print. Printing had ostensibly to take place in Mainz, for on that condition the Archbishop allowed Humery possession of the goods.

All this, it has to be repeated, is speculation. So is the thought that Dr Humery may have been author of the striking opening lines peculiar to the *Catholicon*. There is only a small trail of material evidence that leads to Humery: a manuscript, now in the Biblioteca Apostolica Vaticana, written in his own hand in 1430, which contains lecture notes from the time he was a student in Bologna, was originally wrapped in leaf [n]10 of the *Catholicon*, unrubricated and therefore presumably a leaf of printer's waste.

Printer's waste hints at some intimate involvement in the production of a book: it was material accessible to those connected with a workshop. Traces of printer's waste lead as material evidence to several printers who may have been partners in a consortium. Not surprisingly, we come up first with Peter Schoeffer, who was the only printer active at Mainz at the time. Apart from two instances of printer's waste there is the much stronger evidence of Schoeffer's advertisement of 1470 in which the *Catholicon* is publicized along with many of his own publications and a few probably printed by Ulrich Zell in Cologne. There is, however, also a line of evidence pointing to involvement of Ulrich Zell in the *Catholicon*. There is vellum printer's waste of the *Catholicon* in several volumes bound in Cologne containing Zell quartos. It is likely that there still exists more of this kind of waste than at present recorded. Zell had started his typographical career in Mainz before settling in Cologne in 1464, but there are abundant indications that he maintained some connections with Mainz. Apart from what appear to be Zell titles in Schoeffer's advertisement of 1470, many of Zell's quartos (his speciality) survive bound with quartos printed in Mainz. Outside Mainz Ulrich Zell would therefore appear to be a prime candidate for partnership in a consortium based at Mainz. Finally there may be a connection with Heinrich Keffer, who is known to have worked for Gutenberg, because he is mentioned in the Helmaspergerscher Notarial Instrument of 1455. Keffer was associated with Johann Sensenschmidt in Nuremberg in 1473 in the printing of the *Pantheologia*.

It is now possible to speculate even further. Could it be that they all had some claims on the Gutenberg estate and that by participating in the production of this book, and sharing in profits, they were given the opportunity to redeem some of these claims? Dr Humery may not have been the only one who had to wait patiently to see a return on generosity. If this were the background for a consortium, there would have been a complicated arrangement, because investment was required in the two new paper stocks, in the casting of a large supply of type using the (by then rather worn) matrices available in Gutenberg's shop, and of course in labour. But with the production of books that could be readily sold, financial reward must have seemed assured. The plurality of interests, the size of the investment, would explain a decision to print a larger number of copies than usual; this would be an incentive (but possibly not the only one) for the ambition to produce an impeccable text.

At present I see no grounds, not even for speculation, as to where the presses that produced the *Catholicon* were sited. I can only observe that the peculiarities of the presswork show no relation at all to any known Mainz printing of the period. The complicated arrangement which entailed the well-planned division of work over presses, and the steady transportation of made-up pages of a carefully corrected text, may have led to necessitate the measure of securing the lines and the columns with wire as they were built.

Perhaps the slow unravelling of material evidence may have set us on the trail of an emerging feature in the trade of printed books. We may see here a reaction to restrictions decreed by the authorities – probably with the best of intentions – but running counter to the developing relationships forged by the craft itself and by its necessity to distribute copies through a network that grew rapidly more elaborate. Protection to an important local trade (as, for example, extended early in the 15th century in Bruges by the St John's Guild to the illuminators of books)[12] did not best serve the interest of printers who had to look mainly beyond the city walls for their trade. The heading 'impressos maguntie' in Schoeffer's book list of 1470, where it is now evident that some were printed in Cologne, points the same way: in the direction of mild deceit and subterfuge *vis-à-vis* authority.

In this light the colophon of the *Catholicon* may be open to yet another level of interpretation. It must be obvious that although a misprint 'M.cccc.lx' for 'lxx' is perfectly possible, and could be supported by precedent, I lean towards the view that the colophon is communicating something in a concealed form. If indeed several printers, no longer citizens of Mainz, were involved in a consortium, it can hardly have been to the liking of the Archbishop who would have had formal grounds for objection. It would be human, at least, if this had not deterred Dr Humery, formerly exiled by him, but on the contrary had stimulated his ingenuity. Could it be that the colophon, while praising Mainz as the place of printing in the traditional formula, is, in an inspired form, deliberately concealing the circumstances and even disguising the date of production? The date could be read by those in the know as: '. . . in the years that end with 60', by all others as 1460. If so the colophon has been successful in guarding its secret, and since this can only be put as a question, the secret can still be considered safe.

Every interpretation of history is a product of its own time, and I can see this to be the case with the interpretation of the *Catholicon* colophon I present here. I hope that the analysis of its formulation reflects modern awareness that the meaning of a text can function on more than one level, and that there are layers of interpretation: a deeply religious thought, expressing the submission of the creations of humble man to the will of the Almighty, may on another level serve to pull the wool over the eyes of secular authority.

It is naturally possible to elaborate on all three elements which led to this new interpretation of the statements of the colophon and the assessment of the values to be attached to them: material evidence (the divided paper supplies and the two-line mode of production, combined with external evidence for its dating), the awareness of a possible historical context (Mainz in the 1460s) and a particular situation (Gutenberg's death and his estate).

There are several avenues of research open to the incunabulist which I have not explored here (nor in the much fuller treatment of material evidence in the *Gutenberg-Jahrbuch 1989*). For example, not examined on any systematic basis is the 'hand-finish' of the *c.*70 extant *Catholicon* copies. The rubricators' headings in the first section of the book, which were presumably added in the workshop(s) and were executed in a limited number of hands, have so far not been distinguished or documented. The illumination and rubrication of the copies is an indispensable part of the alphabetical section of the book, and exists in all extant copies. Insight into the illuminators' workshops of the Mainz area has made rapid progress in the last ten years, thanks to the work of Prof. Dr E. König. His impression is that so far no copy of the *Catholicon* examined by him appears to be illuminated in the early 1460s. This preliminary observation indicates an avenue of documentation and research that could well be rewarding.

Further insight into methods of production, and especially press-work, in the first fifteen years of printing, including centres outside the Mainz area, will undoubtedly help to place the *Catholicon* in a proper technological context. The study of incunabula has been very slow to develop in this direction, but has started to do so. It is probably superfluous to add that in this, as in all other contextual issues, the question of dating the book is crucial.[13]

References

1. Sir John Mandeville, *Itinerarium*. [Gouda, Gheraert Leeu, 1483–84]. in-4°.
   M.F.A.G. Campbell, *Annales de la typographie néerlandaise au quinzième siècle*, no.1198; *BMC* ix, p.37.
2. A.F. van Iseghem in his study *Biographie de Thierry Martens d'Alost, premier imprimeur de la Belgique,* Malines, Alost, 1852, connected the book with Thierry Martens and took the colophon as proof of Martens's early residence in Venice. For the subsequent stages of the identification of the place of printing and the printer of the Mandeville and related books see: Wytze and Lotte Hellinga, *Henry Bradshaw's Correspondence on Incunabula with J.W. Holtrop and M.F.A.G. Campbell.*, vol.II, Amsterdam, 1978, pp.485–89.
3. Marco Polo, *De consuetudinibus et conditionibus orientalium regionum*. [Latin translation by Francesco Pipino]. in-4°. Campbell, *Annales*, no.1434; *BMC* ix, p.37.
   Ludolphus de Suchen, *Iter ad Terram Sanctam*. in-4°. Campbell, *Annales,* no. 1622; *BMC* ix, p.36.
4. For Reynaldus de Novimagio see *BMC* v, pp.xix-xx and p.252; for his typographical connection with Gheraert Leeu: Wytze and Lotte Hellinga, *The fifteenth-century Printing Types of the Low Countries,* Amsterdam, 1966, p.37.
5. This figure is based on a study of 1,000 books printed before 1501 in early English ownership. Publication of this study is in preparation.
6. Colophon of: Jean Gerson, *Instruction et doctrine de tous chrétiens et chrétiennes*. [Bruges, Jean Briton (or Johannes Brito), *c.*1477]. Campbell, *Annales* no.807, Paris, Bibliothèque Nationale, Rés. D 7780.
7. For the dating of the first book printed in Oxford see: A.C. de la Mare and Lotte Hellinga, 'The *Expositio Symboli* of Rufinus', in: *Transactions of the Cambridge Bibliographical Society* 7, 1978, pp.xxx-209.
   For the most recent discussion of the *Decor Puellarum* see: Martin Lowry, 'Diplomacy and the spread of printing', in: Lotte Hellinga and John Goldfinch (eds.), *Bibliography and the Study of 15th-century Civilisation: papers presented at a Colloquium at the British Library, 26–28 September 1984*, London, 1987, pp.124–46.
8. A.W. Pollard, *An Essay on Colophons*, Chicago, 1905, pp.159–60.

9. Curt F. Bühler, 'False Information in the Colophons of Incunabula', in: *Proceedings of the American Philosophical Society*, vol. 114, 1970, pp.398–406.
10. Johannes Balbus Januensis, *Catholicon*. GW 3182. The literature very briefly summarized here is: Theo Gerardy, 'Gallizianimarke, Krone und Turm als Wasserzeichen in grossformatigen Frühdrucken', in: *Gutenberg-Jahrbuch 1971*, pp.11–23. Theo Gerardy, 'Wann wunde das Catholicon mit der Schluss-schrift von 1460 (GW 3182) wirklich gedruckt?', in: *Gutenberg-Jahrbuch 1973*, pp.105–25. Eva Ziesche and Dierk Schnitger, 'Elektronenradiographische Untersuchungen der Wasserzeichen des Mainzer Catholicon von 1460', in *Archiv für Geschichte des Buchwesens (AGB)*, 21, 1980, Lieferung 5/6, col. 1303–1360. Paul Needham, 'Johann Gutenberg and the Catholicon Press', in: *The Papers of the Bibliographical Society of America* 76, 1982, pp.395–456. Ensuing discussion and further observations in: W.J. Partridge, 'The type-setting and printing of the Mainz Catholicon', in: *The Book Collector* 35, 1986, pp.21–52. P. Needham, 'The type-setting of the Mainz Catholicon: A reply to W.J. Partridge', in: *The Book Collector* 35, 1986, pp.293–304. Richard N. Schwab, 'Some signs of stereotyping of the Yale vellum copy of the Mainz *Catholicon*', in: *Yale University Library Gazette* 63, 1988, pp.8–13. The proceedings of the conference held at Wolfenbüttel, edited by Werner Arnold and Erdmann Weyrauch, were published in *Wolfenbütteler Notizen zur Buchgeschichte* 13, Heft 2, 1988. They appeared when the present article was in proof. Although a few points of detail may require some further discussion, the papers in this collection do not affect the substance of my argument.
11. I am most grateful to Dr H. Claus, Forschungsbibliothek, Gotha, for providing me with two photographs of the inscriptions in the copies at Gotha, as well as further information, and for his kind permission to reproduce them.
12. L.M.J. Delaissé, *A Century of Dutch manuscript illumination.* Berkeley and Los Angeles, 1968, pp.70–74. James Douglas Farquhar, 'Identity in an anonymous age: Bruges manuscript illuminators and their signs', in: *Viator* 2, 1980, pp.371–83.
13. For full acknowledgement of published materials on which this paper is based I refer to the footnotes in L. Hellinga, 'Analytical Bibliography and the study of early printed Books, with a case-study of the Mainz Catholicon', in: *Gutenberg-Jahrbuch 1989*.

I wish to acknowledge here the information and help I received from many friends and colleagues, in the preparation of the extensive paper as well as of this abstract: Mr Nicolas Barker, Dr Martin Boghardt, Dr L. Boyle O.P., Mr R. Browne, Dr H. Claus, Mr John Goldfinch, Dr E. Hertrich, Mr James Mosley, Dr Paul Needham, Dr Margaret Nickson, Mr Walter Partridge, Dr G. Powitz, Professor R. N. Schwab. In the British Library I have reason to be very grateful for technical assistance to Mrs Anne Gilbert, Mrs Jane Mullane, Mr Tony Parker and Mr Hugh Wilman.

On False and Misleading Imprints in the London Book Trade, 1660–1750

MICHAEL TREADWELL

SIX YEARS AGO, under the general heading of author/publisher relations, I spoke to this same conference on 'Swift's Relations with the London Book Trade to 1714.'[1] On that occasion I had, understandably, a good deal to say about Swift's dealings with Benjamin Tooke Jr, the publisher (in our modern sense) whom he first employed in 1701 and to whom he remained characteristically loyal for twenty years. And when I was not talking about Ben Tooke I was for the most part discussing John Barber, the master printer with whom Swift worked so closely throughout almost all of the four last years of Queen Anne's reign, his own most prolific period of authorship. I make no apology for this concentration for, with a tiny handful of insignificant exceptions, Tooke and Barber between them published all of Swift's work, from the *Contests and Dissentions* in 1701 right down to his eventual retreat to Ireland in 1714. However, what struck me as disquieting even at the time was the fact that of the dozens of Swift's works which passed through the two men's hands over that thirteen-year period only two relatively minor ones carried the imprint of Benjamin Tooke and not a single one that of John Barber. What this implies is that if we had had to reconstruct Swift's publishing arrangements on the basis of the works themselves and the imprints they carry rather than from his correspondence, particularly the *Journal to Stella*, we would have got them entirely wrong. This is because the vast majority of the imprints which actually appear on Swift's published works are at worst false or at best misleading, and it has occurred to me many times since 1982 that in deploying a good deal of documentary evidence in the attempt to reveal the actual state of affairs which existed behind the smokescreen of Swift's imprints I was doing only half the job and perhaps not the more important half. What it now seems to me that we need, quite as much as detailed studies of the publishing arrangements of our greatest writers, is a modest beginners' guide to when to become suspicious that the work in front of us may not in fact have been printed by, printed for, or sold by those whose names it bears in black on white and as likely as not, in italics. And with apologies to those of you who need no guidance from me or from anyone else on such a subject that is what I am going to try to provide in this paper.

I should begin by saying what I understand by a false or misleading imprint; and there is no better starting point than W.W. Greg's section on 'The

Interpretation of Imprints' in his 1955 Lyell lectures, a section which begins with the reminder that

> The object of imprints, a term under which we may for present purposes include colophons, is to impart certain information respecting the circumstances in which the material book has been produced and is being distributed.[2]

For Greg, three agents or groups of agents are involved in such production and distribution:

> the capitalist, who finances the operation, and whom we call the publisher; the craftsman, who produces the article, namely the printer; and the tradesman, who undertakes the distribution, in other words the bookseller.[3]

A full and accurate imprint would thus take the form 'Place: Printed by A at A′, for B at B′; and sold by C at C′. Date' where the place, names and addresses, and date are all accurate, and where A, B, and C did in fact print, finance, and sell the work in question. A false imprint I would define as one in which the place or date have been deliberately falsified, or where those named in the imprint either do not exist at all or, if they exist, have no relation to the work concerned. A misleading imprint I would define as one which, while containing actual place, date, names and addresses, presents the information in such a way as to misrepresent, deliberately or not, the actual roles of the various people involved. The distinction is not always very clear-cut and is, in any case, much less important than the endless varieties of fraud of both kinds available and the problem of how to identify them.

Some work has been done on the problem, but less than at first appears when papers with promising titles like 'Investigating false imprints' in the ESTC-based volume *Searching the Eighteenth Century*[4] turn out to be entirely devoted to works written in French, purporting to come from London, and actually originating in France or Holland. Indeed much of what has been written on the subject has been concerned with the single problem of false place of origin, and while this is understandable given the immediate problems which have faced the cataloguing teams of some of the great national bibliographies, it is often less useful to scholars working in more limited fields than a more general approach might be. Accordingly I intend to say very little here about the well-tilled field of false place of origin and to talk instead about the rest of the imprint and the myriad deceptions it may conceal.

I referred a moment ago to the full and accurate imprint, but the sad fact is that this species is almost never found in the wild. Instead, those herds of accurate imprints which we do encounter have all been abbreviated by the omission of some of the possible imprint information we described above. There are two general reasons for such abbreviation. The first is genuine concentration of function such as that reflected in the imprint 'Printed by Henry Hills, near the Waterside in Blackfriars' where 'printed by' means in fact 'printed by, and for, and sold by' Henry Hills. Such total concentration is only found with printers and, in our period at least, generally only with pirates like Hills or interlopers like George Croom, who did not have easy access to the normal distribution networks of the trade. A far more common form of such concentration of function is that of publisher and distributor where 'printed for' followed by a name and address is clearly to be understood as 'printed for and sold by'. The second reason for abbreviation is simple economy where an imprint which might ideally have appeared in the form 'Printed by John Barber on Lambeth Hill, for Benjamin Tooke at the Middle Temple Gate, and sold by John Morphew near Stationers' Hall' appears as merely 'Sold by John Morphew near Stationers' Hall' because that is all the potential customer really needs to know. And we must never forget Greg's reminder that the imprint was intended for prospective customers, not future bibliographers.[5] The important difference between these two sorts of abbreviation is, of course, that in the second, unlike the first, valuable information is lost.

The omission of information from the imprint does not in itself constitute falsification, but experience has shown that it can mislead the unwary even when all of the information actually contained in the imprint is perfectly accurate. One common danger lies in our natural tendency to read into the claims of the imprint an exclusiveness which is not justified in fact; that is, unconsciously to convert an accurate statement such as 'Printed by A' into the false statement 'Printed by *and only by* A'. This is particularly dangerous in a period when shared printing was common and when almanacs, for example, were almost always assigned to different printing houses for different sheets although they almost invariably carried only a single printer's name in the imprint.[6] More dangerously misleading still, however, is the imprint which omits both the printer's and publisher's names, ending in the contracted form 'London: Printed, and sold by C', an imprint which is often interpreted by the uninitiated to mean that C has first printed and then subsequently sold the work in question. On the worst occasions such an assumption may then lead to a lyrical description of C's presswork or ornament stock, to the despair of more experienced bibliographers who know that C was a poor pamphlet-seller who, to borrow Johnson's exasperated phrase, never drove a field, and had no flocks to batten. For the unfortunate truth is that in the period with which we are concerned there are very few imprints which it is correct to interpret as meaning that the named seller also printed the work 'Printed, and sold by' him or her. The only substantial group of such imprints known to me occurs on the works of Quaker printers like Andrew Sowle or his daughter Tace Sowle Raylton, it having been the policy of the Society of Friends that their authorized printers also distribute the Society's works.

You may have noticed in the above example that I was careful always to emphasize the comma after 'Printed' in the imprint 'Printed, and sold by' because with the omission of the comma which *is* occasionally omitted in practice we may be said to have crossed over from the accurate imprint which may mislead the unwary, to the imprint which is, in itself, misleading – though not in this case deliberately so. By far the largest class of such misleading imprints, as we shall see in a moment, is that in which the distributor is described as being the publisher, that in which the imprint describes the work as being 'printed for C' when the truth is that it is merely being 'sold by' him. In this context it is interesting to note that Greg was anxious to deny the existence of any significant number of such imprints, arguing that, at least where Elizabethan books are concerned 'in all normal cases imprints are capable of strict interpretation and generally mean what they say'.[7] The stumbling block in Greg's way, as he was fully aware, was a large number of works described in their imprints as printed for one person when the copyright of the work was known to belong to someone else. For those who define the publisher of any work as the owner of its copyright such imprints are misleading by definition. Greg, however, as you may have noticed above, defines the publisher not as the owner of the copyright, but as 'the capitalist, who finances the operation' and then escapes the difficulty by arguing that when an imprint describes a work as 'printed for B' even when the copyright of that work is known to belong to A it is because B must have financed that particular edition. Greg's resulting conclusion that in the Elizabethan period 'apart perhaps from occasional errors, the form of the imprint strictly represents the trade relationship of the stationers concerned'[8] he supports with evidence too complex to be summarized here and if I find it not entirely convincing it is also true that I know much less about the Elizabethan trade than did Greg. What I do know, however, is that in the late 17th and early 18th centuries there exists a significant body of imprints which do *not* strictly represent the trade relationship of the stationers concerned. In particular there exists a large number of imprints which describe a work as 'printed for' someone who neither owned the copyright nor in any sense financed the operation of its publication.

The clearest evidence we have of the existence of this particular sort of misleading imprint comes, as is so often the case, from John Dunton, a copyright-owning bookseller or, in our terms, a publisher, who frequently issued works bearing other people's names in order to disguise his own involvement with them and then, years later in his autobiographical *Life and Errors* told the entire world exactly what he had done. The two best-known examples are *An Impartial and Full Account of the Life & Death of... Lord Russel* (1684; Wing L3) which Dunton reveals was 'published' (in the then current sense of 'distributed') for him by Caleb Swinnock and which, sure enough, bears the imprint 'Printed for Caleb Swinock at the Trunck in St. Paul's Church-yard, and are to be Sold by most Book-Sellers', and Charles Gildon's *History of the Athenian Society* (1691; Wing G730) which was similarly published for Dunton by James Dowley and bears the imprint 'Printed for James Dowley, and are to be sold by the Booksellers of London and Westminster'. Other examples not specifically mentioned by Dunton are the sermon *Truth will out* (1683; Wing T3167) 'Printed for Tho. Manhood' and *The Parable of the top-knots*) 1691; Wing D2631) 'Printed for R. Newcome', both of which were entered to Dunton in the Stationers' register of copyrights and the latter of which devotes the last of its four pages to an advertisement for eleven other works published by him.[9]

Of the four supposed publishers named in the imprints of these works none were booksellers, three being bookbinders, notoriously the poorest members of the trade, and the fourth, Newcome, a journeyman printer. For two of them, Dowley and Manhood, these were the only works to which they ever put their names, while Swinnock is named in only one other imprint in the entire Wing period and Newcome in two, at least one of those also a Dunton publication.[10] Moreover, only one of the four works even carries an address so that it is absolutely clear that what we have here is not the accidental substitution of 'printed for' for 'sold by' before the name of the normal distributor, but the deliberate use for the concealment of the real publisher of the name of someone who not only was not the publisher, but who in the normal course of events would not even have been involved in the sale of the work.

Dunton's habit of covering his tracks by using the names of friends who had never 'published' anything before and who, for the most part, would never 'publish' anything again seems merely to have been part of his well-known eccentricity, but there was nothing at all eccentric about the general practice which was widespread in the trade. The main difference was that when the rest of the trade (and occasionally Dunton himself) wished to conceal their involvement with a particular work they had recourse to a small group of specialist agents whom their contemporaries called simply 'publishers', but for whom modern scholarship has adopted the term 'trade publishers' to avoid confusion with the modern sense of the word publisher, and on the grounds that it was their function to publish on behalf of the trade.

Having spoken at some length about trade publishers to the Bibliographical Society in 1981 and then written at even greater length about them in *The Library* in 1982[11] I would not take up your time with them here were it not for the fact that news of their existence seems to be spreading very slowly indeed. Less than a week before getting on the plane to come to this conference, for example, I opened an article entirely devoted to John Nutt, one of the two most important London trade publishers of his day and the trade publisher for Swift's earliest works. The author of that article, while convinced that 'What little has been recorded about the Nutt family in recent times is regrettably imprecise [and] embodies reiterated inaccuracies . . . and confusions . . . '[12] was entirely unaware of what it was that John Nutt was actually doing in his shop 'near Stationers' Hall' between 1698 and 1706, or, apparently, that anyone had ever tried to throw any light on the subject.

Let me reiterate briefly then that from about the beginning of the Popish Plot agitation in the late 1670s when pamphleteering and concealment both became the rage, until about the middle of the 18th century, by which time the newspapers had completely altered the market for controversial writing, there existed in London a small group of specialists who, for a fee, would put their names to and handle the sale and distribution of printed works 'tho the property [was] in another person'. Throughout this period there were never fewer than two nor more than five of these specialist trade publishers, the two best-known and longest-surviving businesses being those 'near Stationers' Hall' which was operated successively from 1680 to the 1720s by Randal Taylor (1680–94), his son-in-law John Whitlock (1694–96), Whitlock's widow Elizabeth (1696–98), John Nutt (1698–1706), John Morphew (1706–20), Morphew's widow Elizabeth (1720–22) and Thomas Payne (1722–26), and that 'near the Oxford Arms in Warwick Lane' which was operated successively from the time of the Glorious Revolution until the 1740s by Richard Baldwin (1688–98), his widow Abigail (1698–1713), and the Baldwins' son-in-law James Roberts (1713–1740s). The 1680s also saw the shorter-lived shops of Langley Curtis, of Walter Davis, and of Richard Janeway, while the next burst of activity in the early 18th century gave rise to those of Sarah Malthus, of Benjamin Bragg and his niece Sarah Popping, of Ferdinando Burleigh and his widow Rebecca, and of John Baker, whose business split on his death between his widow Shirley and her successors William Boreham and John Peele on the one hand, and Thomas Warner and his much better-known successors Thomas and Mary Cooper on the other.

I rehearse all these names at length because the presence of any one of them in an imprint in the form 'Printed for [for example] S. Popping at the Black Raven in Paternoster Row' is an almost certain guarantee that that imprint is what I have called a misleading one and that the work on which it appears was actually published (in our modern sense) by someone else – someone the identity of whom in the absence of surviving manuscript evidence, it will be extremely difficult to discover. There are, of course, exceptions to this rule for – like hypochondriacs who fall ill or paranoiacs with enemies – trade publishers did occasionally own copyrights and publish on their own account. And there are also a large number of trade publisher imprints, perhaps a quarter in all, though the proportion varies widely from one to another and over time, which are not misleading at all, being in the correct form 'Sold by [for example] Ferdinando Burleigh in Amen Corner', where the name of the actual publisher is not misrepresented, but merely omitted. This does not, however, alter the fact that, in the absence of specific evidence to the contrary, it is always safest to assume that *any* work bearing the imprint of a known trade publisher was published for someone else.

I noted earlier that the distinction between misleading imprints, such as those I have just been discussing, and imprints which are downright false was not always very clear-cut in practice and I would like to illustrate what I mean as a way of making the transition from the one to the other.

In discussing the misleading imprints employed by John Dunton I mentioned four different men whose names appeared in the imprints of works actually printed for Dunton himself. Two of these men, Caleb Swinnock and James Dowley, were later referred to by Dunton as having issued the works for him and are therefore known to have existed. The other two, Thomas Manhood and Richard Newcome, I believe also to have existed although Dunton's biographer and bibliographer Stephen Parks does not.[13] For him both names are invented and both imprints are thus in his terms 'fictitious', or in mine 'false'. Manhood certainly did exist for Dunton devotes a paragraph to him in the *Life and Errors*,[14] but for Newcome the evidence is far less clear. Judging by Dunton's habit of using very minor book trade figures in such roles I think it likely that he was the Richard Newcome who was apprenticed from 1680 to 1689 to the printer James Astwood, Dunton's 'near Neighbour and Intimate Friend for many Years' who printed 'near Sixty Books' for him, many during the precise period of Newcome's apprenticeship.[15] The fact is, however, that in the absence of an address in the imprint or any surviving documentary evidence, we will never know whether Dunton's imprint refers to a real Richard Newcome or not, whether it is in my terms a misleading imprint or a false one.

The above examples should alert us to one final danger represented by what I have called misleading imprints, namely that they may mislead even the experienced scholar – perhaps particularly the experienced scholar – into believing them to be false when they are not. There was a time, for example, when I would have accepted the existence of a bookseller named William Dolphin without a second thought. By the time I first encountered a William Dolphin imprint of around 1710, however, I had acquired a little learning, and having determined that he was 'not in Plomer' and knowing something of the significance of the Dolphin in book trade iconography and of Samuel Buckley's use of the sign at this very time, I resolved that he was a fraud. He is, in fact, quite real and operated, albeit for a very short time, as a bookseller and bookbinder at the Peacock in the Strand, possibly the same shop later occupied by the celebrated A. Dodd.[16]

For attempting to find the real-life individual behind a name like 'William Dolphin' I can offer no better advice than 'round up the usual sources', with pride of place going, of course, to Don McKenzie's *Stationers' Company Apprentices*.[17] The two suggestions I can make on the basis of my experience with names which did finally turn out to be real are first to pay particular attention to bookbinders, and second not to neglect apprentices and journeymen. In the late 17th century Dunton used binders frequently as we have seen and almost all of the earliest trade publishers also began as binders. And in the 18th century the seemingly suspect 'John Bagnall, near Fleet-street' in 1709 turns out to be the newly-bound apprentice of the printer Andrew Hinde, in Peterborough Court, near Fleet-street, while the equally obscure 'J.H. Hubbard, in the Old Bailey' in whose name *The New*

Dunciad was pirated in 1742 was the equally new apprentice of the printer Abraham Ilive of the Old Bailey, the brother of the pirate ultimately responsible.[18]

As for journeymen, they seem to have been particularly vulnerable to pressure from their masters to let their names stand in imprints both in the 17th and 18th centuries. The name of Nathaniel Thompson's compositor Alexander Banks, for example, appeared in the imprint of a number of works printed by Thompson in the early 1680s,[19] and in the Hanoverian period journeymen's names were often used in the imprints of newspapers in place of their masters', the best-known examples being Samuel Gray for Samuel Buckley on the *Daily Courant*, Doctor Gaylard for Nathaniel Mist on *Mist's Weekly Journal*, and James Purser for Samuel Richardson on the *Daily Journal*.

Where a likely candidate can be found who fits the name the misleading imprint can be positively identified as such. But given the practical – to say nothing of the theoretical – difficulties of demonstrating the *non*-existence of anyone it is always difficult to prove that a particular imprint is false. An acquaintance with the working habits of the trade does, however, suggest a number of clues as to when an imprint is likely to be false and I would like to take some time to set them out and to explain them.

The first and by far the most important of such clues is the address, and not only for the obvious reason that, although it may be difficult or even impossible to determine the existence of a Timothy Atkins in the Strand in 1717, it is a relatively simple task to ascertain that there was no 'Thick-scull-court in Aldersgate Street' around 1710.[20] Perhaps for this reason the inventors of false imprints very often use real place names even when the address is part of a transparent spoof as in the Hindmarsh-sponsored broadside 'Printed for Tom Tell-troth at the Sign of the Old King's Head in Axe yard in King Street Westminster' (1681; Wing A3973A)[21] or Dr James Smith's *Letter from a Friend at J______*... 'Printed for John Creole, in Jamaica-Street, Rotherhithe' (1746). But if the place names in false imprints are often authentic the addresses are not and the clue is the ubiquitous qualifier 'near'. 'Near Packadilly', 'near the Pall-mall', 'near Westminster-hall', 'near the Strand', 'near Holborn', 'near Fleet-street', 'near Fleet-bridge', 'near Ludgate', 'near Stationers' Hall', 'near St. Paul's Churchyard', 'near Aldersgate Street', 'near Cornhill', and 'near the Royal Exchange' are all addresses to be found on the false imprints of works listed in the bibliography of works relating to a single controversy, F.F. Madan's of the Sacheverell affair.[22] The addresses on genuine imprints are intended to help the prospective customer find the bookseller's shop and accordingly where the street is long or the location vague shop signs and precise qualifiers are added as in 'the Star at the corner of Bride Lane in Fleet Street' (Henry Rhodes) or 'the Gun at the West End of St. Paul's Churchyard' (the Brome family). An imprint which combines 'near' with a vague geographical location should always be approached with caution and will generally prove to be false.

Almost as suspicious as the imprint with the vague address is the imprint with a bookseller's name but no address at all. This was the form largely favoured in the late 17th century as the vague address was in the early 18th when the address-less imprint is sometimes found not on clandestine or pirated works, but on fine or large-paper copies where it merely indicates that the copy was for private distribution rather than for public sale. However, in the 1680s and 1690s, as we have seen from our Dunton examples, the address is as likely to be omitted from a misleading imprint where the name is genuine as from one which is completely false.

And finally, to finish with the address portion of the imprint we should note that the false imprint, even when it carries a plausible name and address, almost never includes the supposed bookseller's sign. And when it does it is almost always in the interests of making a transparent joke like 'the Old King's Head in Axe Yard' which we noted above, or that on Aphra Behn's *Hattige: or the amours of the King of Tamaran* which reads 'Amsterdam [sic], Printed for Simon the African, at the Black-Prince in the Sun, 1683' (Wing B4352).

Turning from addresses to the names carried in false imprints we enter a field limited only by the human imagination. Given, however, that many of the imaginations involved in creating false imprints seem in practice to have been extremely limited there are still distinct patterns of naming which can be discerned and described. Ironically the names which seem the most imaginative are also those which, because they are for the most part comic are the least likely to deceive. Thus Harrington's *Censure of the Rota upon Mr Milton's book* was printed by 'Paul Giddy' (1660; Wing H808), *The Petition of the ladies* for 'Mary Want-man' (1693; Wing P1812), and the *Travels of the devel and towser* for 'Roger Catflogger' (1682?; Wing N36). Everyone will have his or her own favourite, my own being the imprint on the half-sheet poem *England triumphant, or the King of France in a violent passion* which is printed in the best spirit of British chauvinism 'for Mounsier de Garlick Pinch at de Tree Flying Frog, in Spiter de Field' (1708?; Foxon E313). My only caution about such imprints is that imprint jokes, like other jokes, are often only funny in context, and many Cambridge men and women might find nothing strange in the imprint 'Printed for C. Heffer, the Royal Exchange' if they did not notice that it appeared at the bottom of a broadside entitled *The Red Cow's Speech to a Milk-Woman*.[23]

The somewhat more serious names employed on false imprints are, as one can imagine, many and various, but for the most part they may be grouped together into five, admittedly overlapping, categories which I will call commonplace names, deformed names, disguised names, real names, and stock names.

Of the five, commonplace names account for the largest number of imprints including all the most boring and I confess that, even as an inveterate collector of false imprints, I find that I can scarcely bring myself to record another 'J. Smith, near Fleet Street'. However, precisely because names like Smith and Jones,

Brown and White, Thomson and Johnson are so common there were almost always real printers and booksellers with these names in London at any period and therefore, although we may know that a large number of Smith imprints are false, it is often extremely difficult to be sure which ones they are. David Foxon, for example, who knows as much about the Augustan book trade as anyone alive, distinguishes eighteen different London Smiths in the 'Index of Imprints' to his great Bibliography of *English Verse 1701–1750* and feels the need to preface the entries with a note which warns that

A number of Smiths were in business in Cornhill and the Royal Exchange, and may well have been related; they appear to include A., B., E., & M. Smith .... Some of these imprints may be false.[24]

And since there are also D., G., H., J., R., T., and W. Smiths listed in Foxon it is in fact extremely likely that the majority of Smiths listed are ghosts. Ironically, the probability is that it was *because* there were already a number of Smiths active in the London trade that the name was so frequently employed in false imprints, which brings us to our second class of false names, namely deformed names.

By a deformed name I mean one which, although slightly altered, clearly intends to suggest an existing name, the most celebrated example being the 'A. Dob' for 'A. Dodd' imprint on the *Dunciad Variorum* piracies of 1729. This category overlaps somewhat with the former because although one can be sure that A. Dob has been adopted to suggest A. Dodd, one can never be sure whether 'John Brown, in the Strand' has been invented because there was in fact a Jonas Brown in the Strand, or simply because John Brown is an extremely common name. Trade publisher names like Baldwin, Baker, or Cooper which were commonplace as well as conspicuous were particularly likely to be imitated, but for the most part deformation was associated not so much with simple anonymity as with piracy so that the false name could not be chosen at random, but had, like Dob/Dodd, to imitate the name which had appeared on the original. Thus the Sacheverell agitation gives rise to G. Clemants, H. Clemants, H. Clevens, and T. Clements all in honour of the Doctor's official publisher Henry Clements of St Paul's Churchyard.[25] And Hugh Amory, who has also noted the same phenomenon, writes, in connection with a pirated edition of Fielding's *The Mock Doctor*, that 'One of the curious features of English piracies is their tendency to parody the names of genuine printers and publishers: "J. Wells" substitutes for "J. Watts", "C. Borbet" for "C. Corbett", "T. Doddesley" for "J. Dodsley", etc.'.[26] Nor was the practice restricted to the imprint for it was the same desire to parody the genuine for profit which led to Curll's promotion of the poetry of 'J. Gay', who on closer inspection turned out, of course, to be 'an empty Joseph for a John'.[27]

Any suggestion that what we are dealing with here is a sudden rash of misprints should be rejected out of hand, for such deformations were a well-known trick of the trade and one about which the trade was extremely sensitive. John Dunton, for example, was hauled before the Court of the Stationers' Company in 1691 by the irate printer Bennet Griffin who, complaining that Dunton

had printed a Pamphlett called the Magpie [*recte The Parable of the Magpies*] in the name of B: Griffitts wch being soe near his name he Suffered by its reflecting on him, Mr. Dunton affirmed that it was the mistake of the Printer in the printing of B: for W: at the first, but it had since been rectifyed.[28]

The irony, of course, was that W. Griffitts was no more the real publisher than B. Griffitts, though it seems (*pace* Parks) to again be an example of Dunton's using the name of a young journeyman printer, in this case William Griffitts who had completed an eight-year apprenticeship with Bennet Griffin himself only eighteen months earlier – which may explain how Griffin had got wind of what was going on.[29] The degree of sensitivity on the subject can perhaps best be illustrated in a case drawn from periodical publishing and first noticed by Michael Harris in which Francis Clifton warns the readers of his *Oxford Post* of 6 January 1718 against a projected piracy by the printer James Read:

I'm credibly inform'd this Grand Pirate Printer designs to invade my Right, by Printing and publishing a Paper by the Name of the Oxford Post, as also that he'l put at least the two First Letters of my Name to it, and get the same Figure at the Frontispiece; I have therefore only this to beg that my Readers will give themselves the trouble of looking that my Name be Right Spelled and at full length, at the Bottom of the first and last Page, for if one Letter thereof differs from this Present Paper, you may assure your selves the whole is spurious.[30]

Disguised names are those which, while seemingly plausible in themselves, in fact serve to hide another name, real or invented. The archetype of the disguised name is, of course, the anagrammatical name and a good example is 'Charles Tebroc' (for Corbet) which appears on a number of imprints at the time of the Exclusion Crisis.[31] Another very different example may be taken from the very beginning of our chosen period, the year of the Restoration itself, in which six works were published bearing the imprint 'Printed for Charles King'. All were concerned with the events of the time and bore titles like *The loyal subjects tears* and, according to Morrison's *Index* to Wing, they are the only items which carry the imprint of Charles King in the entire Wing period. I have looked at them all and none of them has an address, which makes me almost certain that the imprint is intended to be read 'Printed for', that is 'on behalf of', Charles *the* King. Significantly enough 1660 is also the year in which we find the only known imprints bearing the names of two otherwise unknown members of the Prince family, Augustus and Charles.[32]

The preoccupation with the King in 1660 was natural enough, but different times give rise to different disguises, and the very end of our period offers another sort of disguise entirely in the notorious imprint 'Printed for G. Fenton in the Strand M. DCC. XLIX.' which graced the first edition of John Cleland's *Memoirs of a woman of pleasure*, better known as *Fanny Hill*. This is a bibliographic anniversary of sorts since it was exactly 25 years ago, in the Winter 1963 number of *The Book Collector* that David Foxon offered conclusive evidence that 'G. Fenton' was actually Fenton Griffiths, himself probably a cover for his brother, the bookseller Ralph Griffiths, in the publication of the book.[33] Not that this form of disguise was at all original for Concanen's lampoon on Pope, the *Miscellany on Taste* of 1732, had already used the imprint 'sold by G. Lawton, in Fleet street', an obvious reversal of the name of Pope's then bookseller Lawton Gilliver. Disguises, of course, are not usually so obvious. Many will be impenetrable at this distance in time and many more which may arouse our suspicion will never be subject to proof. David Foxon, for example, thinks that the imprint 'Printed for C. Charters' on a poem of 1730 is 'possibly pseudonymous'[34] while I think that it refers to the infamous Colonel Francis Charteris, but neither of us is likely ever to be able to offer conclusive proof of our hypotheses.

As these examples demonstrate, dating is important where spotting false imprints is concerned and I think that it accounts for another set of what I believe to be false imprints dating from the time of the Popish Plot and Exclusion Crisis. These are the 30 imprints on works all 'Printed for' T. Davis or Davies which appear in the years 1680 to 1682, the first imprints to carry these names since 1662 and the last in the Wing period. The earlier T. Davies imprints had been those of the bookseller Thomas Davies whose career was so usefully set out for us by Charles Rivington in *The Library* in 1981.[35] Thomas Davies gave up bookselling about 1662 upon inheriting a substantial fortune, went into City politics, was knighted in 1667, and in 1677 became the first bookseller Lord Mayor of London. He died in March 1680 the best-known Stationer of his time, and it is a hunch of mine that the T. Davies who published so much from 1680 until the joke wore out in 1682 was, in a more literal sense than usual, the ghost of Sir Thomas Davies.

When we come to consider real names we are again reminded that the line between categories is an extremely fine one, for if I am right about 'T. Davies' then it could almost be considered a real name rather than a disguised one. Sir Thomas Davies was dead, however, and could not have published the works which carry the 'T. Davies' imprint. The real names in the false imprints I am talking about, on the other hand, are those of actual printers and booksellers who were then active in the trade and who could well have printed, published, or sold the works which carry their names, but did not in fact do so. I should emphasize that I am not here talking about the real names of the apprentices or journeymen employed in misleading imprints with their connivance for purposes of concealment. Rather I am concerned with the deliberate employment of another printer or bookseller's imprint on a work without his or her consent and for purposes of deceit. Because the resulting imprints are thus genuine ones which are only false in context they are the hardest of all to identify and we depend almost exclusively on surviving external evidence for their unmasking.

A frequent employer of such false imprints, but fortunately one frequently unmasked, was the printer Nathaniel Thompson who, at the height of the Exclusion Crisis, printed and distributed violently anti-Whig propaganda bearing the imprint of the two leading Whig pamphlet dealers of the time, Benjamin Harris and Langley Curtis.[36] Both Harris, in print, and the authorities, in court, identified Thompson as the responsible party, but failing such evidence we should have no way of knowing that the works in question were not genuine Harris or Curtis productions. Internal evidence might make us suspicious, but internal evidence is already highly problematic where authorship is concerned, and where it relates to the publisher is next to useless. Mark Goldie, in an important paper on the pamphlet literature of the Allegiance Controversy which followed the Glorious Revolution of 1688, has shown that Richard Baldwin, the leading Whig trade publisher of the time, nevertheless sold one Tory tract for every two Whig ones he handled in the controversy, and that the leading Whig bookseller, Locke's publisher Awnsham Churchill, actually issued nearly twice as many tracts classed by Goldie as Tory as he did Whig ones.[37] Into such a stew of political miscegenation it would be foolhardy to venture, though it is intriguing to wonder if some enterprising Tory member of the book trade was not following Nat Thompson's example and using Baldwin's or Churchill's names in imprints without their knowledge or consent.

We come finally to what I have called stock names, by which I mean names that had become so widely established as false that they became a standing joke within the trade. The great continental prototype who coincidentally emerges at just about the time of the Restoration is 'Pierre Marteau', generally of Cologne though he was widely travelled and appears in a number of other places including, apparently, London, though even that imprint claims 'Cologn'.[38] The London book trade seems to have been slower to settle on such a public scapegoat, though the proliferation of 'T. Davies' imprints in the early 1680s which I noted above looks almost like an early, brief flirtation with such a name, suddenly dropped for no obvious reason.

At about the beginning of the Hanoverian age, however, there eventually appeared the celebrated Moore family of imprints, of whom the two best-known were J. and A., although several other letters of the alphabet and every possible variant spelling of the family name are also known. The first Moore to appear in the century, apart from a perfectly legitimate Southwark printer named Thomas, was J. Moore, whom the ESTC credits with two published items in 1713. 1714, however, was definitely the *annus mirabilis* of the Moores as J. was joined by the obviously related A. and the total number of Moore imprints jumped to 40. This

ARS PUNICA.
Pars Altera.
OR,
Truth Vindicated
FROM THE
MISREPRESENTATIONS
OF THE
Dean of *Worcester.*
BEING
A Faithful Collection of Ecclesiastical-PUNS, QUIBBLES, GRÆCISMS, and CONUNDRUMS, extracted from Dr. *Hare's* late conceited Answer to the Bishop of *Bangor*; wherein he has made a May-game of RELIGION, and left the CHURCH a *standing Jest.*

By PHILALETHES.

In former Times Divine Religion *shone,*
(Before these Puny, quibling Tricks *were known,)*
In brighter Splendour, and with clearer Rays,
When ev'ry Pastor *sought his* Maker's *Praise;*
But now Divinity's the Doctor's Part,
And circumscrib'd by empty Rules of Art.
Hobbes's Eccl. Hist.

LONDON,
Printed for *A. Moore,* and Sold by him (under the ROSE) near St. *Paul's.* 1721. Price 6 *d.*

Title page of Philolethes, *Ars Punica* (1721) with the false imprint of A. Moore. British Library, 109.g.45.

vogue seemed destined, however, to be as short-lived as that for T. Davies as the number of Moore imprints dropped to three in 1716 before reviving with the arrival of B., E., M., and T. Moore. By the end of the decade the name had been used more than a hundred times with A. Moore emerging the clear favourite and the total was to reach several hundred by the mid-century with a particular flowering in the 1720s and early 1730s.[39] Clearly something in the name amused the trade and in 1720 the A. Moore who published *Duke upon duke* took newspaper space to warn customers of unauthorized piracies,[40] while in 1721 one Moore even acquired a shop sign, the *Ars Punica* being printed for and sold by him in that year 'under the ROSE' near St Paul's.

So cautious a breed are bibliographers, however, that as late as 1973 a series of notes in Terry Belanger's *Bibliography Newsletter*, while leaning heavily towards the falseness of the imprint were still prepared to conceive of the possibility of a real A. Moore, perhaps the wife of the printer John Moore, active from the 1720s to the 1760s. And this in spite of the fact that David Foxon produced two decisive pieces of contemporary evidence, one from the Cholmondeley (Houghton) MSS noting that 'It must be premised that the name of the printer is on these occasions omitted & A. Moor near St. Paul's generally put where the law directs the printer's name to be', and the other from the bookseller in Fielding's *Author's Farce*, who reveals that 'as the lawyers have John-a-Nokes and Tom-a-Stiles, so we have Messieurs Moore near St. Paul's and Smith near the Royal-Exchange'.[41] This then is perhaps the time to affirm that, in the reigns of the first two Georges, the presence of the name of Moore in an imprint is strong *prima facie* evidence of its falseness, and that Moores should only be assumed to have existed where there is clear documentary evidence of such existence – as, for example, the binding of apprentices or the registering of copyrights in the Company's registers. Smith near the Royal Exchange, *pace* Fielding, is more problematic given the number of real Smiths there and elsewhere, but W. Webb 'near the Royal Exchange' or 'near St. Paul's', or elsewhere, is another stock name of which to beware, surpassing even Moore in the last decade of our period.

Being reminded of the habitual caution of the bibliographer I hasten to close – but to close with an example. In the 1982 treatment of Swift's publishing arrangements which I mentioned at the outset I was careful to account for every distributor's name (pirates explicitly excepted) which appeared in the imprint of any of Swift's works up to 1714 and, indeed, for every name of any kind but one. Had I been asked at the time I would certainly have replied that I had omitted that one because it was not the name of a distributor, but of a ghost, but I can see in retrospect that I cautiously refrained from saying so then, even in a footnote, because I could not *prove* that it was the name of a ghost. The name is that of William Coryton, and it appears in the imprint of the first edition of what is perhaps Swift's most vicious personal satire, the *Short character of his Ex. T.E. of W., LL of I__* 'London: Printed for William Coryton, Book-seller, at the Black

Swan on Ludgate-hill. 1711.' The imprint is unremarkable with a specific address, a plausible sign – indeed one used by the great Whig firm of Awnsham and John Churchill nearby in Paternoster Row – and a name which is neither commonplace, deformed, disguised that I can see (though it is an anagram of Con-Tory), nor, certainly, stock. In short it defies all the guidelines which I have sketched out above. And yet I believe it to be a false imprint, in part because on such a work it ought to be, and in part because I have never been able to find a real William Coryton selling books on Ludgate Hill or elsewhere in 1711 or at any other time. There is, however, a bookseller named Croyton in Ipswich in 1734[42] which is just close enough in time, place, and orthography to keep me from pronouncing myself on William Coryton yet awhile. One can never be too careful with false imprints.

References

1. Subsequently published in the conference proceedings, Robin Myers and Michael Harris, eds., *Author/Publisher Relations During the Eighteenth and Nineteenth Centuries* (Oxford: Oxford Polytechnic Press, 1983), pp.1–36.
2. W.W. Greg, *Some Aspects and Problems of London Publishing between 1550 and 1650* (Oxford: Clarendon Press, 1956), p.82; hereafter cited as Greg.
3. Greg, p.84.
4. Jim Mitchell, 'Investigating false imprints', in Michael Crump and Michael Harris, eds., *Searching the Eighteenth Century* (London: The British Library, 1983), pp.43–58. A similar example from an earlier period is Denis Woodfield's promisingly-titled *Surreptitious Printing in England 1550–1640* (New York: Bibliographical Society of America, 1973) which in fact restricts itself to works surreptitiously printed in French, Italian, Spanish, and Dutch. It is also worth noting that Mitchell's definition of 'false' also differs substantially from mine. For example, he considers imprints in the form 'Londres, et se trouve chez . . . ' where the work has in fact been printed on the continent, but where the seller's name and address are authentic, to be 'not false, since all but the word "Londres" is true' (p.49).
5. Greg, p.82.
6. See, for example, Cyprian Blagden, 'The Distribution of Almanacks in the Second Half of the Seventeenth Century', *Studies in Bibliography*, 11 (1958), 112, note 14. A particular danger here is, of course, that ornaments in parts of a work produced by a secondary printer may be assigned to the printer named in the imprint with the result that errors of printer attribution proliferate endlessly.
7. Greg, p.89.
8. Greg, p.86.
9. John Dunton, *The Life and Errors of John Dunton* (London: S. Malthus, 1705; repr. New York: Garland, 1974), pp.343–4; hereafter cited as Dunton. For Dunton's publications see Stephen Parks, *John Dunton and the English Book Trade: A Study of His Career with a Checklist of His Publications* (New York: Garland, 1976), hereafter cited as Parks,

especially Appendix 3. 'Pseudonymous Imprints', and the chronological numbered Checklist in which the four items cited are nos. 33, 152, 25, and 131.

10. Paul G. Morrison, *Index of Printers, Publishers and Booksellers in Donald Wing's Short-Title Catalogue* (Charlottesville, Va: Univ. of Virginia Press, 1955), hereafter cited as Wing, *Index*.
11. Michael Treadwell, 'London Trade Publishers 1675–1750', *The Library*, 6th series, 4 (1982), 99–134, the conclusions of which are summarized in the two following paragraphs.
12. John Horden, '"In the Savoy": John Nutt and his Family', *Publishing History*, 24 (1988), 5.
13. Parks, pp.405, 201, 203.
14. Dunton, pp.341–2. Identification is admittedly hampererd by Dunton's consistent misspelling of the binder's name which was actually Manwood, and by the fact that Manwood was a member of the Drapers' rather than the Stationers' Company.
15. Dunton, p.326. For Newcome's apprenticeship see D.F. McKenzie, *Stationers' Company Apprentices 1641–1700* (Oxford: Oxford Bibliographical Society, 1974), no.85.
16. See, for example, Dolphin's advertisement of his services as a binder in Luke Milbourne, *A True Defense of Henry Sacheverell, D.D.* (London: W. Dolphin, 1710), p.16.
17. D.F. McKenzie, *Stationers' Company Apprentices 1605–1640* (Charlottesville, Va: Bib. Soc. of the Univ. of Virginia, 1961); *Stationers' Company Apprentices 1641–1700* and *Stationers' Company Apprentices 1701–1800* (Oxford: Oxford Bib. Soc., 1974 and 1978); hereafter cited as McKenzie, *1605–1640*, etc.
18. For Bagnall see, for example, D.F. Foxon, *English Verse 1701–1750* (Cambridge: Cambridge Univ. Press, 1975), W241, hereafter cited as Foxon, and McKenzie, *1701–1800*, no.3959. For Hubbard see Foxon, P791–2, H.P. Vincent, 'Some *Dunciad* Litigation', *Philological Quarterly*, 18 (1938), 285–89, and McKenzie, *1701–1800*, no.4331.
19. G.M. Peerbooms, *Nathaniel Thompson: Tory Printer, Ballad Monger and Propagandist* (Nijmegen: Katholieke Universiteit, 1983), pp.10, 81, 83–4; hereafter cited as Peerbooms.
20. Atkins' name at this address (he also appears elsewhere) occurs on a pirated edition of Swift's *Argument [against] the Abolishing of Christianity* (Teerink 606); Thick-skull-court occurs on the anonymous *Fool's paradise; or, Dr Sacheverel's new hospital for loggerheads*... (London: Bartholomew Booby [!]), no.977 in F.F. Madan, *A Critical Bibliography of Dr. Henry Sacheverell*, ed. W.A. Speck (Lawrence: Univ. of Kansas Libraries, 1978), hereafter cited as Madan, *Sacheverell*.
21. For this Thompson-printed broadside, Thomas Ashenden's *The Presbyterian Pater Noster*, see Peerbooms, pp.58, 68.
22. See note 20, above. It should be noted, however, that although the imprint 'For J. Morris near Stationers' Hall' on Madan, *Sacheverell*, no.81 is false, the same address occurs on hundreds of genuine imprints in the period as that of the Taylor-Whitlock-Nutt-Morphew-Payne trade publisher's shop.

23. British Library, 876.m.19(36).
24. Foxon, II, 178.
25. Madan, *Sacheverell*, nos.251, 280, 994, 121.
26. *New Books by Fielding: An Exhibition of the Hyde Collection* (Cambridge, Mass: Houghton Library, 1987), pp.19–20.
27. Ralph Straus, *The Unspeakable Curll* (London: Chapman and Hall, 1927), p.78.
28. Stationers' Company, Court Book F, 9 February 1691, quoted in Parks, pp.203–4.
29. Parks, p.259; McKenzie, *1641–1700*, no.1800.
30. Quoted in Michael Harris, *London Newspapers in the Age of Walpole* (London: Assoc. Univ. Presses, 1987), p.142.
31. The Wing *Index* lists all Corbet and Tebroc items under Corbet; the Tebroc items are all those for 1682, D2332A of 1683, and B1759A of 1684.
32. Wing C3034, C3127, K547. 'Charles Gustavus' is another similarly suspect name which occurs in more than a dozen imprints in and around 1660. The King's name in particular was disguised in a wide variety of forms and, for example, *The case of Anthony, Earl of Shaftesbury* (1679; Wing C883) 'Printed by K.P. for C.R.' I would read as 'Printed by the King's Printer for Carolus Rex'.
33. D.F. Foxon, 'John Cleland and the Publication of the *Memoirs of a Woman of Pleasure*', *Book Collector*, 12 (1963), 476–87.
34. Foxon, L235.
35. Charles Rivington, 'Sir Thomas Davies: the first bookseller Lord Mayor of London', *The Library*, 6th series, 3 (1981), 187–201.
36. Peerbooms, pp.59–61.
37. Mark Goldie, 'The Revolution of 1689 and the Structure of Political Argument: An Essay and an Annotated Bibliography of Pamphlets on the Allegiance Controversy', *Bulletin of Research in the Humanities* (Winter, 1980), 493.
38. *M. Colbert's ghost*. Cologn, chez Pierre Marteau (1684; Wing M2456). For 'Marteau' see Léonce Janmart de Brouillant, *Histoire de Pierre du Marteau Imprimeur à Cologne* (Paris: Quantin, 1888; repr. Geneva: Slatkine, 1971) and for evidence of his occurrence at Amsterdam, Rotterdam, and Villefranche as well as Cologne see the name and place indexes in V.F. Goldsmith, *A Short Title Catalogue of French Books 1601–1700 in the Library of the British Museum* (Folkestone: Dawsons, 1969–73).
39. The information on Moore imprints in this paragraph which derives from the ESTC file, and which I owe to the kindness of Robin Alston and Michael Crump, was current as of the end of November 1988.
40. Norman Ault, *New Light on Pope* (London: Methuen, 1949), p.186.
41. See Pat Rogers, 'The Phantom Moore' in *Bibliography Newsletter*, Vol.1, No.11 (Nov., 1973), 9–10, with a further contribution by David Foxon in Vol.1, No.12 (Dec., 1973), 6–7 and a running commentary by Terry Belanger to both.
42. 'Mr Croyton in Ipswich' is one of the sellers named in the imprint of Charles Le Brun, *A method to learn to design the passions* (London: for the author [*recte* translator], 1734).

Paper pirates: the alternative book trade in mid-18th Century London

MICHAEL HARRIS

'NECESSITY HAS NO LAW', might stand at the head of this essay as it did at the top of one of the unstamped newspapers published in London during the early 1740s. The notion that it contains a deliberate flouting of conventional authority through a mixture of need and inclination is a useful one in this context. It should be said at once that this piece will not contain a technical discussion of copyright although a general notion of the rights of literary property is central to the argument. My aim is to suggest the existence of a polarisation within the London book trade. I have to admit that this runs partly along lines of wealth and poverty. However, more importantly, the division can be identified in terms of alternative commercial practice as well as opposed views of the rights of competition. Conflict between sectors of the London trade was conventionally presented as a confrontation between legitimate and illegitimate interests with criminality of sorts on one side and respectability on the other. This was certainly how the respectable trade itself, buttressed by other branches of the establishment, liked to define the conflict centred on the issue of literary property. As the struggle developed around the area of publishing, the terms 'piracy' and 'pirate' became part of a one-way traffic of abuse by which members of the respectable trade sought to stigmatize all forms of aggravated competition. The reality was not so simple. It might be worth noting at this stage that literal piracy, like other activities defined by the legal process, was not precise in its broader associations.[2] On one hand, nautical piracy could refer to brutal acts of robbery by water for which the established punishment was confinement in the Marshalsea Prison and a public hanging at Execution Dock. On the other hand, it also carried a more relaxed and populist sense of privateering, of semi-legitimate attack by private individuals against a usurped authority. In the 1730s in particular, as the half-hearted war with Spain was beginning to crystallize around casual conflict at sea, the duality of meaning must have been reinforced. In trying to identify the principal literary pirates and to locate them within what I am calling an alternative book trade I have kept this sort of ambiguous relativity in mind. I certainly do not wish to present either of the nuclear protagonists in heroic terms but to include a notion that the pirates could, on occasion, display some of the buccaneering tendencies of their salt-water counterparts, particularly when confronting the top-heavy galleons of private monopoly.

Before pursuing the pirates, or 'outsiders' as I think they can also be described, I will briefly consider the position of the 'insiders', the printers and booksellers who formed the nucleus of the respectable trade. By the 1730s the tottering structures of external protection had more or less collapsed.[3] The end of the Licensing System in 1695 had removed the underpinning to the authority of the Stationers' Company and the attempts to shore it up through the Copyright Act of 1710 proved strikingly unsuccessful. Indeed, the existence of the Act itself cast a doubt over established ideas about perpetual copyright. Expensive to apply and riddled with loopholes, the legislation protecting the pre-1710 copies wore out in 1731. Attempts to reconstruct an equivalent proved an increasingly forlorn hope.[4] There remained, however, a network of categories of print formally protected by Royal or other grant and the Stationers' Company, the King's Printer, the House of Lords and the proprietors of the Old Bailey Sessions Papers, for example, claimed a variety of exclusive publication rights.[5] For the rest of the respectable trade, defending literary property became largely a matter of commercial self-help. The Law continued to offer one line of defence against interlopers. Injunctions were regularly granted in Chancery against reprints of works whose ownership was claimed by members of the respectable trade. The willingness of the court to support such actions was described by A.S. Collins as 'a strange bias of the juridicial mind'.[6] In reality, of course, legal, political and commercial interests chimed together in a perfectly conventional way.

Operating through a quite tightly organized system of partnerships or 'congers', the members of the respectable trade carved up the right of copy into shares whose transfer was carefully monitored and policed from within. I have argued elsewhere that the move into ownership of the main London newspapers represented both an extension of this system and even, in some cases, a replacement for it.[7] Both before and after the terms specified in the Copyright Act the insiders continued to attempt to buttress their private commercial transactions by entering copies in the Stationers' Company registers and/or by obtaining a Royal Licence under Letters Patent. The rehearsal of the full apparatus of *de facto* legitimacy fills large areas of parchment in the Chancery records.[8] A routine case in point was laid out by John Walthoe and five partners in 1736 during an action against Robert Walker for reprinting Nelson's *Companion for the Festivals and Fasts of the Church of England*.[9] The submission detailed the stages by which the property had passed from the author to the bookseller Awnsham Churchill who, in 1719, sold this and other copies to Walthoe and his associates for £2,200. There followed a long account of the subsequent deaths and replacements of members of the original group as well as of the formation of new partnerships which had led to a widening of interest in the shares. The *Companion* had been entered by Churchill in the Stationers' register a few days before the sale in 1719 and was currently assessed by the shareholders as their most valuable property – worth about £600. The crux of their claim was that this self-contained process, originating from the author himself, was part of the custom and practice of the trade and that on grounds of equity the Walthoe conger should be allowed to enjoy the exclusive benefit of their investment.

The almost Biblical sequences of inheritance and purchase which supported the mid-century injunctions give some sense of the embattled character of the respectable trade. Attacks on literary property came from all directions and defensive action was often needed against rival but equally respectable clusters of shareholders.[10] At the same time, not all the prominent booksellers of the period were securely placed as insiders. Thomas Astley was one of those whose interest in the publication of abridgements, not least through the *London Magazine*, placed him in uneasy juxtaposition to the charmed circles. According to a commercial rival Astley 'in Haste to be rich . . . having very little Property in Copies of Worth, sought to make himself a Sharer, *at the easier* Rate, in those of others'.[11] Astley had, it seems, put himself beyond the pale and could therefore be lumped with the prolific publisher James Hodges who, as a 'Dealer in Ballads and Penny Histories' and hence 'in the lowest Degree of Trade',[12] could also be represented as an outsider.

Who then were these outsiders? Who made up the heterogeneous group circling around the respectable trade in a usually predatory manner, forming what I wish to call an alternative book trade? In the broadest sense they included all those individuals, mainly printers, who were attempting to sustain an independent existence as publishers and who were engaging in every stage of the production, distribution and sale of material. Lacking the corporate resources of the respectable trade, the outsiders were heavily reliant on those forms of output which required the lowest level of initial investment. Consequently, newspapers represented a crucial support and many of the names in this sector, Mist, Applebee, Read and Parker among others, were proclaimed by the 1720s on the mastheads of cut-price weeklies and tri-weeklies.[13] Closely linked to this form of publication and to some extent growing out of it were the more general serials admirably described by R.M. Wiles. From early in the century chunks of literature, history and religion were issued either through the newspapers themselves or as separate part-works. As Wiles has shown, this new approach to publishing, which cut costs to both producer and consumer, spread right across the trade. Among the respectable booksellers gigantic projects based on weekly or monthly publication of a few sheets and organized by such hard-core insiders as the Knaptons dropped heavily onto the market. To take a single example from the 1720s, Fleury's *Ecclesiastical History* was issued monthly by a partnership of fourteen booksellers over a period of five years. Anyone with the staying power to complete the sequence would have ended up with five large volumes containing a total of 3,600 pages.[14] However, paticularly after 1730, serial publication in all its guises became the staple of the output of the pirates, the flexibility of the form not only cutting

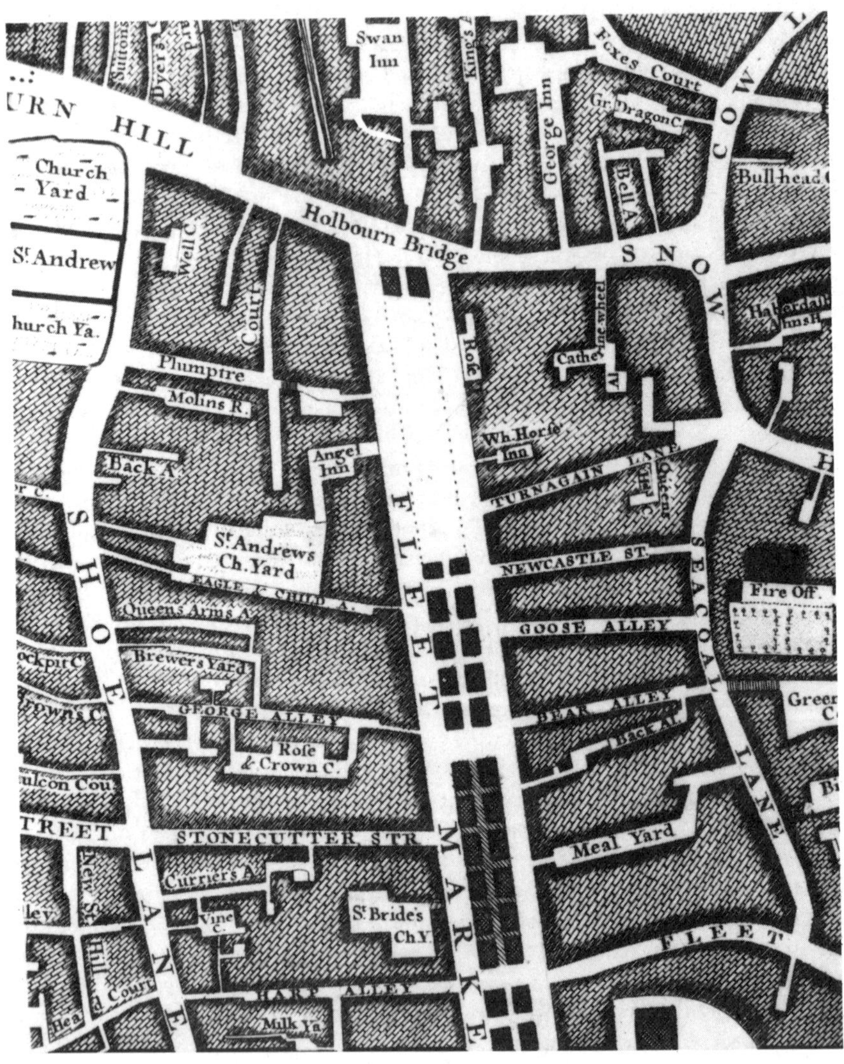

Extract from John Rocque,
A Plan of the Cities of London and Westminster and Borough of Southwark (1747).
Robert Walker's shop was on the corner of Turnagain Lane
and next to the White Horse Inn (1734).

costs but providing viable access to copies claimed by the respectable trade.

The broad definition which I have suggested for the alternative trade needs to be refined further. Not all the independent publishers working in London during the 1730s and 1740s can be so neatly classified.[15] As might be expected the individuals who made up the core of this sector are hard to identify. They certainly cannot as yet be added up or tabulated. The general use of false or misleading imprints, the obscurity of much of their output and the deliberate covering of tracks makes investigation in this area peculiarly difficult. However, a variety of shared characteristics give some sort of cohesion to the printer/publishers working below or outside the circles of the respectable trade. Most were in low if not desperate financial circumstances and a high proportion had some experience of imprisonment either for libel or debt or both. The environs of the major prisons, north and south of the river, formed geographical epicentres of the alternative trade and the area lying between Newgate and the Fleet and within the Rules of the King's Bench in Southwark provided the locus for much of the literary piracy of the mid-18th century. The population of both areas, hemmed into a network of courts and alleys, was to some extent characterized by the presence of the printer/publishers themselves as well as by the immense, open-access prison communities and the numerous pox doctors, usually available after dark. In fact the lines of demarcation were often blurred. Some of the members of the alternative trade worked from inside the prisons while most had an interest in the wholesale and retail distribution of medicines – particularly in specifics for the cure of venereal disease. 'Quackery' was part of the old-fashioned mixed economy within which the outsiders continued to work during the 1730s and 1740s. Few of the core group of pirates had lasting connections with the Stationers' Company and those that did formed part of a dissident splinter group within it.[16] There is a general sense among the members of the alternative trade of a commitment to views and opinions which ran directly counter to those propagated by the new men of the Walpoleian élite. The flavour of Jacobite intrigue and religious extremism hangs over this sector of the trade. It may not be too far-fetched to suggest that the division in the book trade between insiders and outsiders formed part of the broader fissure which ran through the centre of London's political and economic life and has been represented by E.P. Thompson as an incipient class split.[17]

If the individuals at the centre of the alternative trade are hard to pin down in detail it is harder still to establish lines of mutual engagement. Competition in this area was as fierce as among the members of the respectable trade but at the same time evidence of cooperation occasionally shows above the horizon. In the legal formulas of the Court of Chancery 'confederacy' among the pirates was routinely asserted and, although as routinely denied, links between the outsiders were clearly more than a figment. The evidence for this is concentrated around the cut-price and unstamped newspapers which provided an organizational focus for their output. The term 'piracy' in its broader sense could be applied to the unstamped news material itself, published in defiance of the tax authorities under flags of convenience or necessity. Even within this shady area there seems to have been a clear sense of solidarity. In 1740 it was claimed that the proprietors had set up a bank to defend the hawkers of their publications who were under prosecution by the Stamp Office.[18] If this was anywhere near the truth it suggests a level of cohesion comparable to that existing among the radical proprietors of the 1820s. It is through the advertising sections of the cheap papers, stamped and unstamped, that some of the links between the printer/publishers begin to emerge.[19] The individuals whose names seldom, if ever, crop up in the respectable press and who only appear in isolation on occasional imprints are clustered together in this setting. Through the mist the vague configurations involving various Applebees, Reads and Ilives, among many others, loom up giving a heightened sense of reality to the notion of a separation of interest and practice, and hence of an alternative trade.

At the centre of this sector of the business during the 1730s and during part at least of the decades either side, stand the enigmatic but powerful figures of William Rayner and Robert Walker who will provide the main target for the rest of this paper.[20] Not much is known about either personally. The names are common enough and it will require a lot of intricate research of the kind perfected by Michael Treadwell to sort out the identity of all the Rayners and Walkers whose interests circle around the fringes of the alternative trade.[21] Both seem to have been trained as printers, both ran pamphlet shops as well as printing offices and both had substantial medical interests. During 1739 and 1740 they each sold Daffy's Elixir, 'a certain Cure (under God) for most Distempers', from what in both cases was described as the Elixir Warehouse, Rayner's in Southwark and Walker's in Fleet Lane.[22] Walker in particular dealt in the most notable cure-alls and his distribution networks and marketing techniques for print and medicine were clearly interchangeable. The two men must have shared book trade interests but it is almost sublimely difficult to pin down the connection. In the late 1720s William Rayner signed an affidavit on behalf of Walker[23] and the imprint of an anti-Walpole poem, *The Dunghill and the Oak* [1728], read 'printed for R. Walker and W.R.'. It is hard to get much further than this. Perhaps the best indicator of a link lies in the timing and shape of their respective careers. During the late 1720s and early 1730s Rayner and Walker were locked together in the minds of the authorities, as well as in the market, as printers and publishers of opposition material. In 1732 Rayner was arrested for a libel against the administration, tried by a Special Jury consisting 'only of Gentlemen of good Estates'[24] and imprisoned in the King's Bench. Although Walker, who was arrested for the same item, was not brought to trial the prosecution marked a change of direction for them both. Rayner obtained the Rules and moved his printing office to Falcon Court and from the mid-1730s both he and Walker were engaged in the publication of cut-price newspapers and miscellaneous serials on an increasingly large scale. Subsequently their paths diverged, Walker becoming increasingly concerned with provincial trade while Rayner, of necessity, worked the London market. The extent to which their output presented a challenge to the respectable trade was partially revealed by Wiles, although he insisted on characterizing Rayner as a 'pathetic' figure[25] and missed one large category of Walker's output. This arose from his acceptance of the reality of James Stanton, printer and distiller at the sign of the Empty Gallon-Pot, who appeared on the imprint of a growing number of serials from 1736. From evidence in Chancery and elsewhere it seems that Stanton was a fiction, a semi-humorous device, possibly a borrowed name, used by Walker to focus attention on the unpopular Gin Act and perhaps to confuse the Stamp Office.[26] Taking this into account about 30% of the items listed by Wiles in his Short Title Catalogue of serials can be linked to either Rayner or Walker. When this is extended by the output of other individuals who can be classified as outsiders the reality of a division in the structure of publishing becomes clearer.

Through the overlapping careers of Rayner and Walker it is possible to trace the opposed faces of the respectable and alternative trades and to suggest a confrontation of commercial ideology. Much of the literary piracy in this sector was of the 'necessity has no law' sort. Individual printer/publishers simply relied on their own obscurity and the indifference of the respectable trade. In any case, much of their output was aimed at a different level of the market. Such popular material as the chapbooks and ballads which supported the London Bridge publishers, as well as an unknown number of small printers scattered around the fringes of the City, was of no interest to the prosperous cartels. However, confrontation over literary property was possible even at this level. In 1742 Daniel Lynch, described in the subsequent Chancery case as a pedlar, entered into negotiations with Jacob Ilive, then working as servant or agent for Mrs Ellin Akers in Aldersgate Street.[27] Lynch wanted 750 copies of the new *Dunciad* Book Four to be bound up with some of the Pope-Swift correspondence. Ilive agreed, ran off 1,000 copies and was then apparently amazed to find Alexander Pope falling on him from a great height. In a detailed and humble answer to the court Ilive emphasised that not only had none of the copies been sold to the booksellers but that as publication of this material had taken place eight months before, its reprinting had not represented a challenge to Pope's consecutive publishers Cooper and Dodsley. Ilive clearly wished to establish that he was working outside the framework of the respectable trade. Even so, it was a rash act to publish anything which challenged the rights of the most notable living author hardened by years of conflict with Edmund Curll.

Although the publishing activities of members of the alternative trade lay to some extent outside the orbit of their respectable counterparts, this did not imply any general acceptance of the rights claimed under perpetual copyright or royal grant. In the injunction cases in Chancery such denials were built into the formulas of complaint – the defendant being routinely said to give out in speeches 'that he would issue the book as if he owned the copy'. The surviving answers suggest at most a highly sceptical view of the claims of trade monopoly and when two of the Ilive brothers came up against John Baskett as King's Printer in 1741 their response to his recital of privilege can only be described as contemptuous.[28] The fullest expression of opposition to the respectable trade is represented by the clash over the publication of Shakespeare's plays in the mid-1730s. This material, never of course assigned by the author, could be and was seen as a 'Copy that lay in common'.[29] On the strength of this view Robert Walker began, in the Autumn of 1734, to issue a serial reprint of the plays as the first part of a much larger theatrical project.[30] In adopting this sort of specialist output at his office in Turn-again-Lane he was following his preferred commercial technique of head-on collision. It must have been evident that the perpetual copyright of Shakespeare's works was claimed by the respectable trade and that it was one of the most profitable commodities held by their archetypal representative Jacob Tonson.[31] Walker may have had some support among the pirates and Rayner who had personal links with the theatre was obliquely implicated. He had already been active in printing and publishing current plays including Fielding's *Welsh Opera* and had been described, perhaps by Fielding himself, as a 'notorious Paper Pyrate'.[32] In August 1734 a correspondent of Tonson identified as one of the main encouragers of Walker's 'Pyratical Edition' a Mr. Gardner 'who reprints for that scandalous Fellow Rayner in the King's Bench'.[33] The details of the Shakespeare dispute have received some attention but partly because of gaps in the record it has not been identified as a clash between opposed sectors of the trade.

Walker began to publish the plays weekly at the low rate of *4d*, so undercutting the previous Tonson editions which had sold at 1/- each. The course of the ensuing conflict was charted by Walker himself in a series of printed notices issued seperately as handbills or published with his plays. According to this account, supported at various points by sworn affidavits, the initial response of Tonson and his main associate William Feales followed what was to become a routine pattern. After waiting for Walker's edition to run out of financial steam an attempt was made to buy him off. Later in the decade John Osborn was given a private pension for not publishing an edition of Shakespeare and on this occasion Walker was offered a contract for printing work worth at least £200 a year if he would drop his series.[34] The offer was rejected and Tonson and Feales turned to threats of prosecution. In a letter to Edward Cave, who in 1745 proposed his own annotated edition of Shakespeare, Tonson displayed the slightly sinister smarminess that was probably applied to Walker. 'As you are a man of character', he wrote, 'I had rather satisfy you of our right by argument than by the expence of a Chancery suit... '.[35] Walker was more resilient than Cave, and Tonson and Feales were finally obliged to resort to commercial brute force. They began to exploit their financial muscle by undercutting Walker himself. A new weekly

ADVERTISEMENT.

WHereas, *R. Walker*, with his Accomplices have printed and publish'd several of *Shakespear*'s Plays; and to screen their Innumerable Errors, advertise, That they are Printed as they are Acted, and industriously report, that the said Plays are printed from Copies made use of at the Theatres; I therefore declare, in Justice to the Proprietors, whose Right is basely invaded, as well as in Defence of my self, That no Person ever had, directly or indirectly from me, any such Copy or Copies; neither wou'd I be accessary on any Account in imposing on the Publick such Useless, Pirated, and Maim'd Editions, as are publish'd by the said *R. Walker*.

W. CHETWOOD, Prompter to His Majesty's Company of Comedians at the Theatre-Royal in Drury-Lane.

THE

PURITAN:

OR THE

WIDOW

OF

WATLING-STREET.

By Mr. WILLIAM SHAKESPEAR.

LONDON;

Printed for J. TONSON, and the rest of the PROPRIETORS; and sold by the Booksellers of *London* and *Westminster*.

MDCCXXXIV.

ADVERTISEMENT.

J. Tonson, and the other Proprietors of the Copies of *Shakespear*'s Plays, designing to finish their Edition now publishing, with all Speed, give Notice, That with the last Play they will deliver *Gratis* General Titles to each Volume of the whole Work, so that each Play may be bound in its proper Place: And also do give further Notice, That any Play of *Shakespear*'s that now is, or hereafter shall be out of Print, will be reprinted without Delay; so that all Gentlemen who have bought those Plays, shall not be disappointed, but may depend on having their Sets compleated.

N. B. *Whereas one* R. Walker *has proposed to Pirate all* Shakespear's *Plays, but through Ignorance of what Plays are* Shakespear's, *did in several Advertisements propose to print* Oedipus King of Thebes *as one of* Shakespear's *Plays; and has since printed* Tate's King Lear *instead of* Shakespear's, *and in That and* Hamlet *has omitted almost One Half of the Genuine Editions printed by* J. Tonson *and the* Proprietors; *The World will therefore judge how likely they are to have a compleat Collection of* Shakespear's *Plays from the said* R. Walker.

THE

PROLOGUE.

THE doubtful Title, Gentlemen, prefixt
Upon the Argument we have in Hand,
May breed suspence, and wrongfully disturb
The peaceful Quiet of your settled Thoughts:
To stop which Scruple, let this brief suffice,
It is no pamper'd Glutton we present,
Nor aged Counsellor to youthful Sin;
But one, whose Virtue shone above the rest,
A valiant Martyr, and a virtuous Peer,
In whose true Faith and Loyalty exprest
Unto his Sovereign, and his Country's weal:
We strive to pay that Tribute of our Love
Your Favour's Merit; let fair Truth be grac'd,
Since forc'd Invention former Time defac'd.

A 2 Dramatis

Notices published in the Tonson edition of Shakespeare attacking Walker. The lower illustration is from *The Life and Death of Thomas Lord Cromwell* (1734).

edition of the plays was initiated each selling at *3d* to the public and *1d* to the hawkers. At the same time, in order to make this confrontation more effective, Tonson and Feales attempted to suborn one of Walker's workmen to provide details of his order of publication so it could be duplicated. Walker's response to each of these moves was violent and public. First, he totally rejected all notions of a Shakespeare copyright, describing Tonson's rehearsal of share transactions as 'a long Detail of a Cock and a Bull'.[36] 'The Duumverate', he wrote, 'have the Impudence to say they will apply to Parliament for an Act to secure their Properties: a fine thing indeed! to imagine that the Parliament will grant them a Property to which they never were entitled; let them take my Advice for once, that is to think what ill Use they made of a former Act by holding Books at ten times their Worth.' In the same notice he defied Tonson and Feales to go to law 'for what they have no Right to, why don't they do it? Here is Term come, and no Bill in Chancery, no Action at Common Law.' Walker continued to throw out his challenge and to heap abuse on what he described as Tonson and Feales's 'piratical edition' describing their texts as 'maim'd Scraps'. He also continued to publish his plays in defiance of 'the Body of Booksellers who vainly oppose this Undertaking' and, in fact, stepped up his weekly publication rate issuing plays by Shakespeare and other authors through three retail outlets.[37]

However, in his second line of attack against the Tonson-Feales partnership on grounds of personal sharp practice he over-reached himself. He was certainly not, as he put it 'one of those poor Noodles who would be frightened by their insolent Threats', but he went too far in the opposite direction and laid himself open to a prosecution for libel in the Court of King's Bench. This arose directly from his printed notice issued soon after the publication of the first of the Tonson-Feales cut-price plays.[38] In it Walker sounds apoplectic with rage. 'I can't call you Gentlemen', he wrote, 'but Fools. I believe the World will think terribly of you when they consider what a vile thing it is to entice a Servant or otherwise to betray his Master's Secrets. If you have anything to say to me call on me. I am at home in a Morning till 11 O'Clock and I'll give you such Satisfaction as you Deserve.' In his address to the public he again returned to the attack. Denouncing 'those Monopolising Creatures Tonson and Feales', he went on to urge the public that 'as I have freed you from Oppression it is to be hop'd you'll stand by and support me while nothing but Death shall be the hindrance of my persevering in what I have promised.' The threat of an action in the King's Bench was as serious as the price war and was bound to lead to substantial expense. None-the-less, Walker remained bullish. 'These mighty Men think, that by their great Purses they shall be enabled to pull Mr. Walker down, but Mr. Walker is a Man of Resolution, and such they'll find him, who will not be frightened by their insolent Threats.' In the event, Walker completed his Shakespeare series but seems to have given up his more comprehensive theatrical project – at least for the time being. This may have been the direct result of the King's Bench action at which he was

THE

LIFE

AND

DEATH

OF

Thomas Lord *Cromwell.*

A

TRAGEDY.

By *SHAKESPEAR.*

LONDON:

Printed by R. WALKER, at *Shakespear's*-Head, in *Turn-again Lane*, by the *Ditch-side.*

M DCCXXXIV.

Title page of the Walker edition of
The Life and Death of Thomas Lord Cromwell (1734).

found guilty, perhaps spending a short time in enforced proximity to Rayner.[39] It certainly did not purge him of his view of perpetual copyright and for the rest of his career he continued to flout the claims of the respectable trade in general and the Tonsons in particular.

One of the reasons for dwelling on the Shakespeare conflict is that it hinges on opposed notions of piracy and the free market, juxtaposing the attitudes of insider and outsider in a particularly forceful way. Another reason is that it helps to demonstrate the reliance of the pirates on direct, almost personal, links with their readers. When Walker expressed his view of 'liberation retailing' he was clearly identifying how the buoyant market could be exploited to side-step the clutches of the respectable trade. A lot of nonsense has been written about the static demand for print in this period. It is a view arising mainly from the stale ideology of a few political historians.[40] In fact any limitation on output was the result not of a lack of demand but almost entirely of constraints imposed on supply by the entrenched interests of the respectable trade. As Walker's comments suggest, the survival, and the success, of the pirates was achieved through an extended relationship with the public as consumers rather than through the rock-hard structures of insider dealing which kept the respectable publishers at one remove from the more extreme pressures of demand. The alternative alignment can be identified in most areas of commercial practice. When, in 1739, William Rayner attempted to dispose of a large quantity of his unsold serial works he did so not at one of the carefully monitored trade sales but by the old-fashioned means of a subscription sale to the public. This took the form of a lottery with 8,000 tickets selling at 2/6 each. 'And as a further Encouragement to the *Adventurers*, the first drawn Number will entitle the Owner to a Silver Cup of 10*l*. value; and the last drawn, to a Silver Punch Bowl, Cup and Ladle of the Value of 20*l* over and above the Chances which either of the two Shares may be entitled to.'[41] In this way Rayner presumably hoped to attract speculators from a broad constituency extending well outside the trade itself. This is not, of course, to give Rayner some sort of moral superiority but simply to indicate that he was closer to the reality of the market than most of his respectable counterparts.

Rayner's reliance on public interest in the area of stock disposal was related to the primary need of the alternative trade to establish its own lines of communication within the market. Because of their commercial muscle the powerful, shareholding groups had the capacity to close off or at least obstruct the established distribution outlets which supported publication in the central areas of London and beyond. The mechanisms of intervention bore down most heavily on the mercuries whose pamphlet shops were particularly vulnerable to the respectable trade – as they were to the political establishment.[42] In both cases the newspaper provided the lever for control. Trade influence was exerted, partly at least, through the supply of full-price newspapers on which the livelihood of such mercuries as Anne Dodd and Elizabeth Nutt was largely dependent. Offending the respectable publishers by distributing cut-price newspapers or piratical serials would have been as financially dangerous as selling hard-core political libels. Action against interlopers sometimes took a more direct form, particularly when an outsider was attempting to market a copy claimed by the respectable trade. Publication of Rapin's *History of England* was a major area of contention in the early 1730s and the printer James Mechell, who was trying with consistent lack of success to project a translation by John Kelly, found even the preliminary publicity a problem, "There having been many Persons employ'd to destroy the Proposals wherever they could meet with them; and also intimidate some who would have taken in Subscriptions, by idle Threats of Prosecutions, &c.'[43] Mechell went on to list eleven coffee houses and taverns where information on the project could be obtained. His advertisements appeared in one of the more obscure cut-price papers alongside those of other members of the alternative trade and the existence of a line of open-access publicity was clearly of value in side-stepping some forms of restrictive practice.

Against this background street and direct sales were vital to the outsiders, and hawkers figure prominently in their advertisement for the supply of serials of all kinds. In the London region the members of the alternative trade constructed their own networks of newsmen taking orders for and delivering material around circuits which conventionally extended 40 miles or so from the centre.[44] Walker's plays were advertised as available within 60 miles of town. Agents in the satellite population centres also redeployed the material through their own, sometimes low-key and unrespectable outlets. The only advertisement I have found referring to this process appeared in the cut-price *Penny London Post* in 1744. In it John Moore, probably the 'Puff' Moore arrested the previous year for selling unstamped London papers, announced his services. Describing himself as newsman of Upper Deptford in Kent he offered all the newspapers and 'Subscription Books', as if in London, Daffy's Elixir and a cross section of other medicines. As well as binding books he also sold 'Dutch Pickle Herring, at 2d. a Couple, Spruce Beer at Is. 6d. per Quart, and Flower of Mustard.'[45] It seems unlikely that he would have had much to do with the respectable trade. In fact, it seems possible that Moore was one of Robert Walker's agents and that he was a modest link in a distribution network that extended from London across large areas of Southern England and the Midlands.[46]

The miscellaneous serials and cheap newspapers that flowed through these channels kept the London pirates afloat. There was not much the respectable trade could do about it in legal terms, even though a high proportion of the material was technically second-hand. The printer/publishers, following the line of highest demand and lowest resistance, established long-running sequences which it was particularly difficult for the respectable trade to defend. Abridgements or heavily annotated texts could be issued as new work and the pirates were particularly successful in applying this notion to the religious serials which

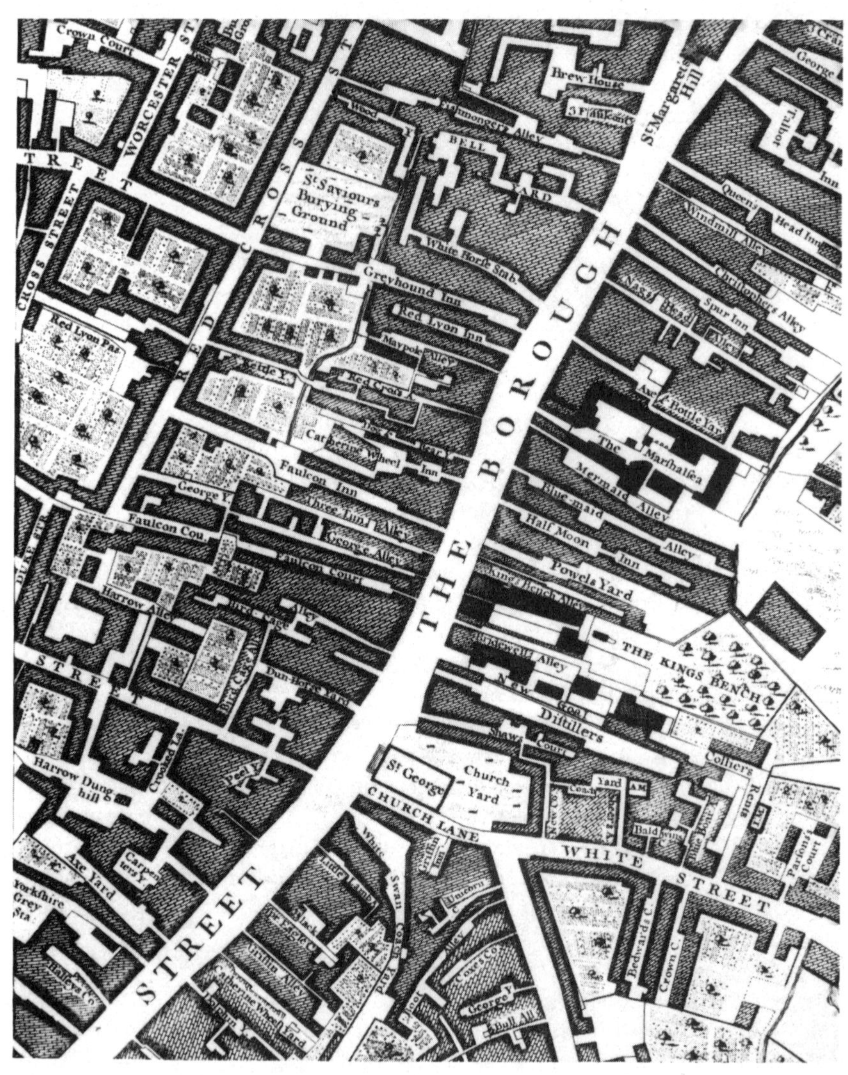

Extract from John Rocque,
A Plan of the Cities of London and Westminster and Borough of Southwark (1747).
From 1733 to 1741 William Rayner's printing office was in Faulcon Court, within the Rules of the King's Bench prison.

formed a substantial component of their output. Many of the authors who were contracted by outsiders were producing massive Biblical commentaries or re-workings of the *Book of Common Prayer* to be issued in serial form. Such items were claimed as a breach of copyright by the King's Printer whose grant under Letters Patent gave exclusive right to the publication of Bibles and prayers. Consequently in the mid-1730s John Baskett was drawn into a brisk engagement with members of the alternative trade. Baskett was highly vulnerable. Being in low, not to say collapsed, financial circumstances, his efforts to contain the challenge to his monopoly were easily swept aside.[47] In 1735 the printer Robert Penny began to issue a heavily annotated Bible in weekly parts. His advertisements claimed that these were available through outlets in Bristol, Exeter, Worcester and Colchester as well as from 'most other booksellers'. After preliminary legal action in Chancery, Baskett, for a fee of £100, issued Penny with a license to publish, imposing a number of restrictions on the quantity and timing of his edition. Shortly afterwards both were back in court, Baskett claiming that Penny had exceeded the terms of the agreement as well as negating its spirit by his hard-sell publicity. Penny, on the other hand, claimed to have discovered that Baskett, or his associates, had been negotiating a second deal with William Rayner then engaged in the production and sale of his own 'family Bible'.[48] Whatever the outcome it seems clear that Baskett was holed below the waterline. Both Rayner and Walker recycled large chunks of Biblical material during the 1730s and 1740s annotated by in-house or freelance authors, issuing the material in separate sheets or with cut-price newspapers.[49] It evoked some very hostile responses in the respectable press. 'Amongst the licentious practices', wrote a contributor to the *Grub Street Journal*, 'by which this Nation is distinguished at this time [1736], from all the Nations of the World; I am persuaded, nothing can equal the audacious Liberty which some have lately assumed in printing the sacred Oracles of the living God without any Authority or Privilege . . .'[50] Even so, no action seems to have been taken in Chancery against either Rayner or Walker for this sort of piracy and Rayner's religious serials, congealed into massive tomes in the British Library, suggest a long-term and profitable enterprise. At his death in 1761 a quarter share in his illustrated Bible, annotated by the elusive Dr Smith, was valued at £87.[51]

The challenge to the King's Printer was one of a series of pragmatic moves against respectable monopoly in mid-century. Walker in his head-on conflict with Tonson and Feales over the Shakespeare copyright was attacking the flagship of the respectable trade. Both his personal visibility and the strength of his ideological commitment were out of the ordinary. The pirates were usually active at an altogether more opportunistic and surreptitious level. Rayner certainly seems to have been more inclined to pick off the stragglers from the main fleet. There are no indications that, like Walker, he saw himself as a participant in a commercial resistance movement. Nonetheless the nature of his business brought him into confrontation with the respectable trade and his publishing practice challenged conventional notions of competition. This emerges most clearly from his predatory engagement with the newspaper, a form of publication which lay outside any defensible concept of copyright. Titles and formats were duplicated with impunity while the different forms of content ebbed and flowed across a variety of publications evoking, for the most part, only rage and grief.[52] Commercial force was the best defence against piracy and it was the opportunity of plundering one of the less well defended publications on the fringes of the respectable trade that brings Rayner's commercial organization briefly into view.

Described in 1740 as '*one of the most notorious Pyrates of this Age*'[53] his office in the Rules of the King's Bench became the focus for a motley collection of outsiders. These included the printers Abraham Ilive, his brother Jacob, also a type-founder and literary forger imprisoned in the Marshalsea for debt in 1738,[54] and Doctor Gaylard whose imprints in the early 1730s carried the slogan 'some Time Resident in the King's Bench'. Among the several very obscure authors on his payroll the most visible was Dennis de Coetlogan who described himself as Knight of St Lazare, M.D. and Member of the Royal Academy of Angiers. His links with Rayner may have begun in 1737 with the setting up of an unpopular political newspaper called the *Alchemist*. This collapsed under prosecution and catapulted Coetlogan into Newgate with dire personal results.[55]

From his enforced base in Southwark, Rayner seems to have organized raiding parties across the river. Using portable presses, hiring rooms and borrowing identities from within the trade, his activities and those of his employees and associates are very hard to pin down.[56] During the late 1730s he seems to have been stalking the opposition newspapers looking for a way into one of the most profitable areas of the market. His chance came at the end of 1737 when the management of the *Country Journal: Or, the Craftsman*, a successful weekly not owned by one of the powerful clusters of respectable shareholders, went into spasm following an official prosecution for libel.[57]

Convicted of printing and publishing the paper Henry Haines was imprisoned in the King's Bench.[58] He continued to run his Bow Street printing office from the prison and to produce the *Craftsman* but fell out with his principals – the printer/bookseller Richard Francklin and the author Nicholas Amhurst. Finding himself in very low water Haines came to some sort of agreement with Rayner over the running of the paper. As he soon realised it was easy enough to come alongside an experienced newspaper publisher of piratical tendencies but harder to avoid being scuppered in the process. While negotiations developed between Haines and the proprietors, production at Bow Street continued smoothly. The crunch came when a final accommodation was reached and Rayner refused point-blank to drop the paper. As a result two virtually identical publications began to appear on the market, one owned by the Francklin-Amhurst combination and printed by Henry Goreham, the other produced by Rayner under the slightly amended title of the *Country Journal: Or, the Original Craftsman*. The ambiguities of who was doing what to whom in terms of copyright or piracy were considerable. Haines himself foundered while Rayner, probably some time in 1738, set up his own production centre at premises in Chancery Lane. Nominally these were run by the freeman printer John Standen and about the middle of 1739 the whole operation was shifted to the Old Bailey. According to a notice in the paper this was primarily for the benefit of the mercuries and hawkers as the office was now 'within a *few doors* of the *Printer* of the *Daily Post* and *London Evening Post*'.[59]

What gives the case of the *Original Craftsman* a particular interest is that it lifts the curtain on a stratum of surreptitious publishing which was not just a haphazard activity organised by random individuals down on their luck. The *Original Craftsman*, though outwardly a conventional weekly newspaper, was part of the output of an alternative book trade characterized by occasional piracy but with some degree of inner cohesion. The extent of Rayner's interest and the influence of what might be called the Southwark connection, emerges from the statements taken during legal proceedings launched by the authorities in 1739.[60] John Standen and his business manager were both from south of the river and it appears that Standen allowed his name 'to be made use of for the sake of being employ'd by the Proprietor [Rayner] in another Printing House in which the said Proprietor has a share,. . .'.[61] Doctor Gaylard organised the composing and printing and among the other individuals who worked at some time in the office was Mrs Applebee (*née* Blackburn) who was probably connected with the sole witness for Rayner at the time of his prosecution.[62] The paper was written partly by Coetlogan who delivered his inflammatory copy to Rayner's parlour in Falcon Court, and Benjamin Defoe, as ever, in desperate financial circumstances. The entire enterprise has the appearance of one of Rayner's well-organized excursions against the respectable trade and there is every possibility that it followed an established pattern.

The pirates were working right across the London market. All forms of publication were likely to come under pressure and the postures of defence and attack can be identified in most areas of the publishing business. It remains to be asked what happened to this generation of outsiders, particularly Rayner and Walker, and to assess briefly how successful they were at sustaining an independent commercial existence. In Rayner's case the information is, as ever, clouded and contradictory. The sheer range of his output of newspapers and serials suggests a reasonable financial success. He valued the stock of part-works and prints at his subscription sale at £1,502 and at his release from the King's Bench in 1741 he appears to have owned two houses within the Rules.[63] On the other hand, he was prosecuted for debt while in the prison and his petition for release stated categorically that his long-term imprisonment was due to his utter inability to pay a fine of £50.[64] Was Rayner one of those entrepreneurs who were later identified as using the King's Bench as a secure base for their business ventures?[65] Perhaps this will become clear with further research. As for Walker, although his large-scale publishing business seems to have flourished over two decades, there is no indication that it generated a high level of prosperity. In the mid-1750s Judith Walker, perhaps his widow, was still in Fleet Lane publishing low-key pamphlets on crime.

What is clear is that not all the pirates of the 1730s and 1740s were sunk without trace and circumstances outside the trade could produce some curious alterations. Walker continued in business through the 1740s and his edition of *Paradise Lost* was the subject of proceedings in Chancery as late as 1751.[66] Rayner, however, followed a different route. He proved as adept, or fortunate, in manipulating his personal relationships as he was in exploiting his publishing opportunities. According to John Nichols he cheated his two wards out of a substantial legacy in the early 1740s and although this may have been retrospective sour grapes by a commercial insider, in other respects his remarks were reasonably accurate.[67] Apparently, after moving his printing office to Wine Office Court, Fleet Street in 1741, Rayner entered into a liaison with a family whose story was later described as 'a tale of lust, murder, madness and intrigue'.[68] In brief, Sir John Dinely-Goodere was murdered in 1741 by literal pirates hired by his brother who was subsequently hanged. Meanwhile, Sir John's heiress wife Mary, who in the face of her husband's brutality had become 'oblivious to the sacred vows she had taken', was imprisoned during the mid-1730s in the King' Bench. Here she may have met Rayner. At all events, ten years later, in 1743, the two were married. At a stroke Rayner acquired both financial security and, through the purchase of the Lordship of Charlton in Worcestershire, social status.[69] His world was certainly turned upside down and the years of piratical struggle were forgotten. He continued for a while to work as a respectable printer, enrolling apprentices for the first time with the Stationers' Company and applying for a Royal Licence for one of his long-term Biblical serials.[70] Some time after 1744 he sailed away into decent obscurity at Hammersmith.

This is not, I think, entirely irrelevant in an assessment of what was happening to the alternative trade generally. By the mid-1740s the commercial environment in London was hardening and Rayner's *volte face* might have come about in a less dramatic way under normal circumstances. The tightening-up of the tax legislation in 1743 hit the producers of cut-price newspapers and serials hard.[71] At the same time, the increasing homogeneity of the respectable trade, clustered around the successful, full-price newspapers, was bearing down heavily on the outsiders. Walker's increasing interest in provincial work was perhaps a symptom of this. Nonetheless, what I have called the alternative book trade had a functional reality in the London of the 1730s and early 1740s. When in 1739 Walker published his first edition of *Paradise Lost*, in defiance of the Tonson claim, he put on the imprint 'Printed for a Company of Stationers'. It seems to me that this was not just an ironic swipe at the authentic Company but was an assertion of a sort of group solidarity outside that establishment structure. In some respects the London pirates were linked most directly in terms of commercial practice and style with the members of the provincial trade, the *Fratres in Malo* who appear on the cover of this volume. While the London outsiders were being squeezed the challenge to worn-out notions of perpetual copyright was continued in the more distant centres of the trade. To give a final flourish to the overworked metaphor, the London pirates of the 1730s and 1740s can be seen as the vanguard to a flotilla which, sailing on the flood tide of an expanding market, finally blew the monopolists out of the water and ran up the skull and crossbones over a relatively free market in books.

References

1. *All alive and Merry*, dates uncertain but in publication between 1740 and 1743.
2. For a summary of the recent research into crime and the law in English society see Joanna Innes and John Styles, 'The Crime Wave: Recent Writing on Crime and Criminal Justice in Eighteen-Century England', *Journal of British Studies*, XXV (1986), pp.380–435.
3. There is a substantial literature on copyright which includes examination of the post-1695 position. Useful accounts of the legal structure to the middle of the 18th century appear in R.M. Wiles, *Serial Publication in England Before 1750* (Cambridge University Press, 1957), pp.154–62 (Cited hereafter as Wiles, *Serial publication*) and John Feather, 'The Publishers and the Pirates: British Copyright Law in Theory and Practice, 1710–1755', *Publishing History*, XXII (1987), pp.5–32.
4. A.S. Collins, 'Some aspects of Copyright', *The Library* 4th ser., VII (1926–27), pp.67–81.
5. For an account of the arrangements for publication of the *Old Bailey Sessions Papers* see Michael Harris, 'Trials and Criminal Biographies: a Case Study in Distribution', in Robin Myers and Michael Harris eds., *Sale and Distribution of Books from 1700* (Oxford: Oxford Polytechnic Press, 1982), pp.1–36.
6. Collins, 'Aspects of Copyright', p.71.
7. Michael Harris, 'Periodicals and the Book Trade', in Robin Myers and Michael Harris eds., *Development of the English Book Trade, 1700–1899* (Oxford: Oxford Polytechnic Press, 1981), pp.66–94.
8. My systematic use of Chancery material was made possible by R.J. Goulden whose work on book trade cases, 'Some Chancery Lawsuits 1714–1758: An Analytical List', first appeared in *Factotum*, the newsletter of the Eighteenth-Century Short Title Catalogue Project at the British Library, and was issued separately in an extended form in 1983.
9. J. Walthoe v R. Walker, 1737, Public Record Office (P.R.O.), Chancery (C) II/1534/62.
10. See, for example, the account of the struggle over rival translations of Pierre Bayle's

Dictionnaire Historique et Critique in the early 1730s, Wiles, *Serial Publication*, pp.114–17.

11. Advertisement in the *Penny London Morning Advertiser* 156, Friday 27 April 1744.
12. Advertisement in the *Country Journal: Or, the Craftsman* 681, Saturday 28 July 1739. For an account of the scale and range of the London Bridge trade in which Hodges was involved see Margaret Spufford, *Small Books and Pleasant Histories* (London: Methuen, 1981).
13. The development of these publications is traced in Michael Harris, *London Newspapers in the Age of Walpole* (London and Toronto: Associated University Presses, 1987), pp.20–1 (Cited hereafter as Harris, *London Newspapers*.)
14. Wiles, *Serial Publication*, p.100.
15. For example, the publishers of music and also of prints and maps stand in an ambiguous relation to the groups I am describing.
16. This was the case with Jacob Ilive who organised a serious challenge to the Livery of the Stationers' Company in 1762; Cyprian Blagden, *The Stationers' Company: a History, 1403–1959* (London: George Allen and Unwin, 1960), pp.232–33.
17. E.P. Thompson, *Whigs and Hunters* (London: Allen Lane, 1975). The implicit links between the interests of the political establishment and the respectable trade can be identified in his study through the activities of the Treasury Solicitor, Nicholas Paxton. See also Harris, *London Newspapers*, pp.136–38.
18. Petition from Daniel Pratt to the Duke of Newcastle, 2 May 1743, British Library (B.L.), Additional Manuscripts (Add. Mss.) 33,054, ff.189–90.
19. Shared newspaper interests within the alternative trade also emerge from the records of the payment of advertising duty. A. Aspinall, 'Statistical Accounts of the London Newspapers in the Eighteenth Century', *English Historical Review*, LXIII (1948), pp.201–32.
20. For an account of Rayner's interest in the London newspaper press see Harris, *London Newspapers*, pp.90–8. R.M. Wiles provides a substantial amount of information on both in *Serial Publication* and on Walker in *Freshest Advices: Early Provincial Newspapers in England* (Ohio: Ohio State University Press, 1965).
21. Additional information about the career of Rayner as well as many other members of the London trade will appear in K.T. Winkler, *Targesschrifttum und Politik in der Ara Walpole*, in preparation, Göttingen University.
22. Rayner's advertisement in the *Country Journal: Or, the Craftsman* 652, Saturday 6 January 1739 and Walker's in the *London and Country Journal* 52, Thursday 15 May 1740.
23. *Daily Journal* 3147, Friday 5 February 1731. The question arises of whether this is the right William Rayner.
24. *Daily Advertiser* 560, Thursday 16 November 1732.
25. Wiles, *Serial Publication*, p.67.
26. Walthoe v Walker, 1737, P.R.O., C.II/1534/62.
27. A. Pope v J. Ilive, 1742, P.R.O., C.II/837/14.

28. J. Baskett v R. Whitworth, 1741, P.R.O., C.II/1564/4.
29. *Observations on the Case of the Booksellers of London and Westminster* (London: [1774]), p.1.
30. A list of 24 dramatists whose work was to be published by Walker in serial form appeared at the end of the second volume of his collected Shakespeare plays. For Walker's serial publication from July 1740 of *The Beauties of the English Stage* containing a variety of non-Shakespearian material see Giles E. Dawson, 'Robert Walker's Edition of Shakespeare', in Josephine Bennett *et al* eds., *Studies in the English Renaissance Drama* (New York: New York University Press, 1959), pp.77–9.
31. Tonson used the sign of Shakespeare's Head to identify his business and Walker, adding insult to injury, adopted this for his own printing office in 1734.
32. Advertisement in the *Daily Post* 3674, Monday 28 June 1731.
33. Letter from an unknown correspondent to Jacob Tonson, 29 August 1734, B.L., Add. Mss. 28,275, f.319.
34. For Osborn's pension see *Observations*, p.1.
35. [Samuel Pegge], *Anonymiana* (London: 1809), p.34. I am grateful to Joseph Levine for this reference.
36. This and subsequent references are taken from notices in the Walker edition of Shakespeare's plays collected in seven volumes and held by the British Library.
37. His addresses were Turn-again-Lane, Snow Hill (alternatively near Fleet Lane, by the Ditch-side); Change Alley, Cornhill; between the Savoy and Somerset House in the Strand. Towards the end of the sequence the last two locations were dropped.
38. What follows is based on the indictment laid by Tonson and Feales against Walker in the Court of King's Bench, P.R.O., Crown Roll, Hilary 8 George II, King's Bench (K.B.) 28/132. The content of Walker's advertisement which does not seem to have survived elsewhere is quoted in full in the Bill and I have silently removed the legal interpolations.
39. The document ends with a record of the guilty verdict followed by the words 'Let him be taken.'
40. In work which emphasises the static and traditional nature of English society, a reasonable attempt to demonstrate the integrative character of the newspaper press is sometimes unreasonably extended to suggest a low level of demand for all forms of print. For example, Jeremy Black, *The English Press in the Eighteenth Century* (London: Croom Helm, 1987).
41. Advertisement in the *Universal Weekly Journal* no number, Saturday 5 May 1739.
42. For the political pressure placed on the London mercuries see Harris, *London Newspapers*, pp.38–98, 146.
43. Advertisement in the *Universal Spy: Or, Aesop the Fabulist* 3, Saturday 8 April 1732.
44. Harris, *London Newpapers*, pp.40–1.
45. Advertisement in the *Penny London Post: Or, the Morning Advertiser* 204, Friday 17 August 1744. For 'Puff' Moore see Harris, *London Newspapers,* p.41.
46. Seven of Walker's provincial newspapers are identified in G.A. Cranfield, *A Hand-*

List of English Provincial Newspapers and Periodicals 1700–1760 (London: Bowes and Bowes, 1961).

47. In the period 1714–1758 there were 58 lawsuits in Chancery which named John Baskett as principal plaintiff, Goulden, 'Chancery Lawsuits', p.2. He was declared bankrupt in 1728.
48. The negotiations over Samuel Humphreys, *The Sacred Books of the Old and New Testament*, printed and published by Penny during 1735, appear in P.R.O., C.II/1865/24 and 25.
49. For example by Rayner, S. Smith D.D., *The Compleat History of the Old and New Testament: Or, A Family Bible* (London: 2 vols., 1735, 1737); by Walker, the *London and Country Journal: with the History of the Old and New Testament* published in at least two different series between 1739 and 1742. Six of Walker's provincial papers identified by Cranfield were issued with a religious serial identified in the title.
50. *Grub Street Journal* 334, Thursday 20 May 1736.
51. Purchase by Thomas Lowndes from Henry Baldwin of shares in copies previously owned by Rayner, 4 June 1761, B.L., Add. Mss. 38,370, f.11. The continuing publication of religious material by the London printers was acknowledged in *The Speech of Mr Jacob Ilive to his Bretheren the Master Printers* (London: 1750), p.4.
52. For divisions within London newspapers leading to the issue of nearly identical publications see Harris, *London Newspapers*, pp.85–8.
53. *Country Journal: Or, the Craftsman* 746, Saturday 10 October 1740.
54. William Bucknell v Jacob Ilive, P.R.O., Plea Roll, Michaelmas 12 George II, 1738, K.B.122/169.
55. Coetlogan lost an eye in Newgate; Harris, *London Newspapers*, pp.140–41.
56. For the involvement of Doctor Gaylard and Abraham Ilive with the pamphlet bomber Robert Nixon in 1736 and the Pretender in 1745, see Harris, *London Newspapers*, p.96.
57. Harris, *London Newspapers*, pp.125, 144–45.
58. A full, if contradictory, account of the wrangles that followed appeared in the *Country Journal: Or, the Craftsman* 746, Saturday 10 October 1740 and in the *Daily Gazetteer* 1711, Friday 12 December 1740. The *Gazetteer* material was reconstituted in Henry Haines, *Treachery, Baseness and Cruelty Display'd* (London: 1740).
59. *Country Journal: Or, the Original Craftsman* 714, Saturday 13 October 1739.
60. The materials which relate to the prosecution are preserved in P.R.O., State Papers Domestic (S.P.) 36/50.
61. This claim was made in the examination of Benjamin Norton Defoe, 14 November 1739, P.R.O., S.P. 36/50/29.
62. *The Friendly Writer and Register of Truth*, November 1732, p.12.
63. Advertisement offering further details from the printer Henry Goreham in the *London Morning Advertiser* 965, Friday 20 November 1741, *et seq.*
64. Prosecution for debt in William Steele v W. Rayner, P.R.O., Easter 12 George II, 1739, K.B. 122/175. Award to Steele of £5 10s. with three guineas damages. Petition

from Rayner for release referred to Nicholas Paxton, 29 January 1740, P.R.O., Treasury 4/11/175.

65. William Smith, *State of the Gaols in London, Westminster, and Southwark* (London: 1776), p.52.

66. J. Tonson v R. Walker, 1751, P.R.O., C.11/1106/18.

67. John Nichols, *Literary Anecdotes of the Eighteenth Century* (London: 9 vols., 1812–1815), VIII, pp.447–48.

68. Anon., 'Murder Most Foul; Or, the Bristol Fratricide', *Factotum*, 17 (1983), p.16.

69. Although he was said by Nichols to have alienated the property shortly afterwards he described himself in his will, proved 14 November 1761, as a native of Charlton. P.R.O., Probate 11/870.

70. D.F. McKenzie, *Stationers' Company Apprentices 1701–1800* (Oxford: Oxford Bibliographical Society, 1978); petition for Royal Licence for *A Family Bible*, n.d., B.L., Add. Mss. 33,054, ff.215–6.

71. Harris, *London Newspapers*, pp.29–30.

'Et Tu Brute?' History and Forgery in 18th-century England

JOSEPH M. LEVINE

IT MUST HAVE come as something of a shock to discover in 1742 that the well-known correspondence between Brutus and Cicero, which had been read and cited by generations since its discovery in the Italian Renaissance, was just another forgery. The occasion for its unmasking was a formidable new life and times of Cicero by Conyers Middleton, who had relied heavily on the letters for that crucial period in his story when both Cicero and the Roman Republic were tottering toward their final collapse. The critics were two Cambridge colleagues who produced in quick succession two large books to make their point. Middleton did not give in easily, and a quarrel began which lasted for a decade in England and sputtered on for more than a century in Europe.

That another classical work should be called into question was dismaying but not altogether unexpected. By the middle of the 18th century, nearly everyone was aware that scattered among the ancient works – and modern ones as well – were an unknown number of literary frauds and forgeries. Suspicion was rife, fanned by a historical 'pyrrhonism' that had been fashionable for several decades and that called into question the very possibility of reliable historical knowledge. In France, in particular, a controversy raged in which the whole of early Roman history was abruptly discarded and all the ancient testimonies called into question as dependable sources.[1] Meanwhile, an eccentric French Jesuit, Père Hardouin, startled everyone by alleging that almost all the ancient classical works and many of the Church fathers were the invention of a coterie of monks in the later Middle Ages. Although the charge seemed absurd and Hardouin was not left free to develop it, it was taken seriously enough in England to warrant refutation.[2] More specifically, some remembered that Dares and Dictys, those two ancient reporters of the Trojan Wars, had finally been proved the inventions of a much later time, rather than the eye-witnesses they claimed to be; while others recalled the Renaissance forger, Annius of Viterbo, with his mixed bag of ancient writings, including the lost history of Berosus of Babylon, and the terrible mischief that that had caused.[3] Everyone knew about the 'pious frauds' that disgraced the early Christian tradition, from the Sibylline Oracles and Hermes Trismegistus to the letters of Jesus to King Abgarus, and

Paul to Seneca, not to mention many others, though no one could be sure just how many. More than one work was written during the period to show how such frauds and fabrications could be detected.[4] Above all, everyone knew about the recent exposure of the false letters of the ancient Sicilian tyrant, Phalaris, and the fierce quarrel that had ensued.

Let me remind you, for a moment, of that famous event, a story first memorialized by Jonathan Swift in the Battle of the Books and told no doubt again and again in the halls and chapels of Cambridge University. It centres, of course, on the famous Dr Richard Bentley who was recognized throughout Europe as the master scholar of the age, and who ruled over Trinity College with an iron hand until his death in 1742. Bentley had been drawn into the controversy between the ancients and the moderns by his young friend, William Wotton, as the champion of the moderns. Wotton was defending the familiar idea that the moderns equalled or surpassed the ancients in many ways, but he introduced a new argument when he claimed for his side the achievement of modern classical scholarship. In a chapter of his book in 1694, he singled out philology as one of the greatest accomplishments of modern times, an invention of the Renaissance barely known to antiquity.[5] Wotton described the peculiar ability of learned critics to restore correct readings and discover forgotten meanings in the ancient texts, and he claimed that a modern scholar could build a knowledge of antiquity more profound and extensive than any that the ancients could have had. If this seemed a paradox, it was easy enough to demonstrate with a roll-call of modern scholars and their learned works. That this meant much drudgery and a 'pedantry' that was often derided by men of the world, Wotton was willing to concede: poring over old manuscripts, comparing variant readings, utilizing old glosses and scholia, and being 'minutely critical in all the little Fashions of the Ancient Greeks and Romans'. But it seemed to him that the corrections of modern editors and the annotations of modern critics also required a sagacity and keenness of wit that sometimes surpassed the originals. It helped that scholarship was cumulative, like natural science, so that the last was usually the best; but still the scholar 'must have a perfect Command of the Language and particular Stile of his Author . . . a clear Idea of the Way and Humour of the Age in which he wrote'. If so, he could sometimes, 'expose Authors who have had the good luck to be exceedingly commended by learned Men'.[6]

Wotton saw an unexpected opportunity to make his point when Bentley told him one day that his opponent, the 'ancient' Sir William Temple, had blundered foolishly by proposing that the letters of Phalaris were the oldest and therefore the best of their kind. Wotton asked Bentley to write out his objections, which he then appended to the second edition of his book (1697). This aroused Temple's friends in turn, who answered in the name of a young aristocrat, Charles Boyle, in the best way that they knew how, with a brilliant combination of personal invective, witty satire, and faulty scholarship. Now it was Bentley's turn and he hastily put together a massive treatise to demonstrate his original point that the letters were beyond doubt a forgery of later times, the work of a clumsy Greek sophist meant as a school-boy exercise, a work of no literary merit whatever, but a mere 'fardle of commonplaces'.[7]

To introduce his argument, Bentley saw that it would be helpful to describe the extent and abundance of classical forgeries. He had little trouble showing that to counterfeit books and give them to distinguished authors was a practice as old as letters. He quotes Galen in particular to demonstrate that the rivalry of the kings of Pergamon and Alexandria for literary treasures drove up the price of fakes and was 'an Invitation to the Scribes and Coppyers of those Times'. But money was not the only incentive. 'Glory and Affectation' supplied new motives, 'as an Exercise of Stile and Ostentation of Wit'.[8] Here is where the sophists excelled, for it was the ordinary task of the schools to set themes for students, 'to make Speeches and write Letters in the Name and Character of some Heroe, or great Commander or Philosopher'. What would Achilles, or Medea, or Alexander say in such and such a circumstance? One sophist confessed that he had written some answers to Brutus in Greek as a trial of skill; but most of them concealed their names and put their imitations forward as originals – and succeeded before a gullible audience.[9] But the variety of fakes was inexhaustible. 'What clumsie Cheats, those Sibylline Oracles now extant, and Aristeas's Story of the Septuagint,' not to mention the moderns: Annius of Viterbo, or that notorious Inghirami, who had pretended to discover the works of Etruscan antiquity in 1637. All were easily exposed, but all had had defenders. Occasionally, Bentley was willing to allow a more difficult case, like the fake *Consolatio* ascribed to Cicero but skilfully forged in the 16th century; more often it was like the recently discovered Petronius, so badly bungled as to be a 'scandal to all Forgeries'.[10]

With Phalaris, the case was obvious. To Bentley, the letters revealed themselves immediately as just another in a whole class of forgeries. A couple of years earlier, he had warned the Oxford Professor of Greek, Joshua Barnes, against the epistles of Euripides, only to be publicly rebuked for his impudent lack of judgement when the works of the dramatist appeared.[11] Bentley was only too happy for the opportunity to demonstrate now that those letters, as well as others attributed to Themistocles and Socrates, were exactly like those of Phalaris, the forgeries of inept sophists. They were among many more of their kind that had once been attributed to Anarcharsis, Democritus, Hippocrates, and so on. Bentley promised a large Latin dissertation to refute them all if necessary.[12]

It took the great scholar several hundred pages to dispose of Phalaris; he never bothered to return to the rest. I shall not trouble you with a reiteration of his arguments, except to say that he used his extraordinary command of the whole of Greek language and literature, numismatics, epigraphy and chronology, to pile up inconsistencies and anachronisms of many different kinds, to make his point. Bentley's work did not settle the argument which was obscured by the satire and invective of 'Boyle' and Swift and the rest, and went on merrily for a generation. But his *Dissertation* furnished a model of critical scholarship for all who cared to see, and it won gradual acceptance and eventual admiration, even against the derision of the wits. Meanwhile, Bentley's reputation grew at home and abroad with a succession of critical works and further controversies in which he tried to restore the corrupt texts of many classical authors, the *New Testament*, even Milton's *Paradise Lost*, which he claimed had been tampered with by a mischievous editor.[13] His whole career can be seen as an attempt to apply the critical techniques and methods of modern classical scholarship to distinguishing the true from the false in all the many works of Latin and Greek antiquity. There were few scholars anywhere, and certainly none at Cambridge, who did not feel the influence of this famous man or react to his personality during his long life.

Conyers Middleton entered Trinity College while the battle of the books was in full progress; a few years later he became a Fellow after an interview with the Master.[14] Like many in the College, he grew restless under Bentley's not very benevolent tyranny and joined in a long and not very successful rebellion that began about 1717 and ended only with Bentley's death. It may be that it was this contest that tempered Middleton's Tory politics and turned him into a Whig with a wistful nostalgia for the liberty of the Roman Republic. Be that as it may, Middleton (or 'fiddling Conyers,' as Bentley liked to call him with a sneer)[15] showed himself early a good polemicist with a hatred of dogmatic authority, and he began a war of pamphlets which extended eventually into the realm of scholarship. Middleton had the temerity to challenge the great man's projected edition of the Greek New Testament and to hold his own in the exchange.[16] This brought him a considerable reputation, though his new credentials were hardly the thing to win him preferment. Although he tried, Middleton was never quite willing to acquiesce in that placid respectability that seemed to offer the surest way to success in the 18th-century church. In 1731, he ruined his chances altogether by arguing again, this time with an old Bentleian disciple, Daniel Waterland, a pillar of orthodoxy who had undertaken to defend the Anglican faith against the deist challenge. Middleton believed himself a rational Christian opposed to the superstition of 'Custom, Authority and Interest'. Needless to say, that did not help his clerical reputation, and so he had to settle in the end for the more congenial occupation of man of letters. Not even 'double attendance' at Church each Sunday 'could wipe off the Stain of Infidelity', although Middleton remained eternally hopeful.[17]

The life of Cicero was a shrewd undertaking, nicely calculated to repair the damage and improve his prospects. Cicero appealed to everyone in the 18th century as the greatest orator and prose writer of antiquity, a statesman and philosopher who had played a signal role in some of the most notable and best reported events in ancient history. His rhetoric was taught in the schools; his

Cicero in his book-lined study.
Frontispiece to *Ciceronii Opera* edited by Isaac Verburg (Amsterdam; 2 vols., 1724).
British Library, 656.g.7.

orations and letters were used as models of prose style; his philosophical works were regarded as an encyclopedia of wisdom in all worldly matters; and he could be read by an Englishman in English, French, or the original Latin. When the Duke of Wharton suddenly decided on a parliamentary career, he found that he had forgotten his Latin; so he got Edward Young to go to Winchester with him, 'where they did nothing but read Tully and talk Latin for six weeks – at the end of which [so we are assured] the Duke talked Latin just like Tully's'.[18] Cicero appealed to Middleton in particular for his political principles and his religion. But the great Roman had never yet received a proper biography.[19] Sometime about 1734, Middleton undertook the task, determined to recount in full and exact detail the life and times of his hero. It was a larger job than he anticipated.

Middleton was well-prepared, however; he had been to Italy in 1724–25 and surveyed the scene of the great events for himself. He had collected antiquities and books and brought them back to England. Now he had married into pleasant circumstances and won the patronage of some important men, so that he had the leisure and resources that he required. He was determined to write from the original sources and to include as much of Cicero as possible, 'imagining that his own words would be more affecting to a reader, than by abstract of the substance of them from another hand'.[20] This meant translating and stitching them together, without spoiling the narrative flow. His friend and confidant, Lord Hervey, read every line as it was composed and thought that it was admirably done, the transitions in particular, 'so natural and easy . . . rather a Beauty than a Blemish'.[21] Middleton worked hard at his style which was much admired in his day, by Pope and Gray among others. 'As fast as I endeavor to make it legible and fair, I scratch and blot it again, till I confound both my work and myself'.[22] Trouble with his eyes slowed his progress. As the book grew large, Middleton was convinced that it must be divided into two volumes and sold by subscription. But the army of subscribers that was finally assembled by Hervey and Middleton's many friends was kept waiting impatiently. Even the printing was slow, especially when the paper ran out; but eventually, in 1741, the two volumes appeared triumphantly. 2,001 copies were dispersed at two guineas a copy. The work was an immediate success and was followed by many further editions.[23] Hervey received the flattering dedication (which was quickly parodied by Fielding) and responded generously; from the proceeds, Middleton was able to purchase a modest country estate and imagine a contemplative retirement. He had taken care, he wrote to his friend, Warburton, 'to keep clear of all offense, being disposed to spend the rest of my days in quiet, and to avoid controversy'.[24]

Middleton had meant to write history as much as biography, and he took his precepts as well as his matter from Cicero. In this he followed the fashion, for whenever history was discussed in early modern times, it was Cicero who supplied the commonplaces that were endlessly quoted to endorse the subject for its special value to public life and for its intimate conjuncture with rhetoric and eloquence. Twice Middleton quotes from the *De Oratore* to the effect that the historian must tell the truth without prejudice, relate his story in good order, pay careful attention to motives and causes, and above all employ a clear and agreeable style.[25] Unfortunately, Cicero did not say much about how to dig out the truth, though he was concerned, as a good rhetorician, with the psychology of communication: that is, with the pitfalls of bias and prejudice. But here Middleton could draw upon Renaissance humanism with its increasing insistence upon eye-witness testimony and contemporary documentation, and he saw the peculiar opportunity afforded by his subject in its unique abundance of contemporary materials – especially Cicero's own works. There was, after all, nothing like it in antiquity.[26]

Though Middleton proclaimed his desire to tell the truth objectively, he admitted a predisposition in Cicero's favour, and his inveterate use of Cicero's own language and explanations tended to reinforce this prejudice, though he believed he was only letting the facts speak for themselves. For Middleton, Cicero was the most nearly perfect politician and human being who had ever lived, 'the most accomplished with every talent that can adorn civil life, and the best fraught with lessons of prudence and humility, for all conditions of men, from the prince to the private scholar'.[27] He especially admired Cicero's political principles and the practical role the Roman had played in trying to preserve Republican liberty when all was lost, and this is the leitmotif of his narrative. 'If Rome could have been saved by human council,' Middleton several times insists, 'it would have been saved by the skill of Cicero'.[28] Even when Cicero appeared to vacillate and compromise, Middleton found every excuse to justify his policy: Cicero understood the necessities of political reality and always sought a mean between the extremes of Cato's stubborn but stupid idealism and the easy and flaccid accommodation of his friend, Atticus; between Stoicism and Epicureanism.[29] Cicero, so Middleton wrote to Warburton in 1736, had 'one general, consistent, glorious Character, of a great and good Man, acting and speaking in all Occasions, what the greatest Prudence with the greatest Virtue would suggest'. From that point of view, even Cicero's vanity and love of praise, so often urged against him, could be excused as necessary to the life of a magistrate and statesman.[30] Although the book was warmly received, not everyone was persuaded. As Mrs Donellan found, when she met the Bishop of Oxford one day with his wife and Miss Talbot, everyone agreed that 'Dr Middleton was not so much the historian as the Panegyrist of Cicero'.[31]

Middleton's admiration for the statesman extended also to his 'enlightened' viewpoint. He found in Cicero's teaching 'the most perfect system of Heathen morality, and the noblest effort and Specimen of what mere reason could do towards guiding men through life with innocence and happiness'.[32] Cicero had seen through the superstition of Roman religion, though he recommended it for its civic use as a device to keep the public peace, and he believed in all the important tenets of true religion: God the Creator, the immortality of the soul, etc. (When Warburton denied that Cicero believed in a future state, this led first to a nervous exchange of letters, then, finally to a rupture.) Middleton seems often to anticipate Edward Gibbon, who certainly read his work; nowhere so much, perhaps, than in that beginning passage, where Middleton recalls visiting Cicero's family seat at Arpinum and finding a Dominican convent there. 'Strange revolution! to see Cicero's porticos converted to monkish cloisters! the seat of refined reason, wit and learning, to a nursery of superstition, bigotry and enthusiasm! What a pleasure must it be to give to these Dominican inquisitors to triumph on the ruins of a man, whose writings, by speaking the light of reason and liberty through the whole world, have been one great instrument of obstructing their unwearied pains to enslave it.'[33]

So, Middleton saturated himself in Cicero's writings. He was infatuated especially by the many hundreds of letters that had survived and that gave him peculiar access to the characters and personalities, and the true motives, of his great cast.[34] In them, he could discern too, behind Cicero's public persona, an attractive private man, 'one of the greatest statesmen of the world, cherishing and cultivating in himself the soft and sociable affects of love and friendship'. From the two dozen letters that alone remained between Brutus and Cicero, it was possible to draw a contrast that did much to explain the course of events. Brutus was 'churlish, unmannerly and arrogant'; Cicero, cheerful and steadfast, 'in all respects uniform, great, and glorious'. Cicero alone understood the requirements of the moment. These letters were 'the best vouchers of what I have been remarking, and enable us to form the surest judgement of the different spirit and wisdom of the men'.[35]

Middleton's book was divided into eleven narrative sections and a conclusion, written out and printed in chronological order. It was a vexing job merely to put things in order, though here Middleton was helped by previous editors, from Manutius and Victorius in the 16th century to the recent French translator, Nicolas Mongault.[36] In his preface, he laid the scene with a sketch of the Roman constitution in which he argued forthrightly for the sovereignty of the people. His history was intended to remind his countrymen of the lessons of the past, and his account of the Roman senate was meant to recall the story of the English parliament. Inevitably, it led to controversy, first with his friend Hervey, later with others, and the publication by Middleton of a whole book on the subject in 1747.[37] It seems now that all sides were mistaken, that everyone read back into the reign of Romulus, institutions that were only developed long afterward – much indeed in the way English historians were then reading back into earliest British history the origins of parliament and hereditary monarchy. These anachronisms were perhaps inevitable in the 18th century as a result of what R.G. Collingwood called 'substantialism', the conviction that all human institutions, like all human personalities, appear to have a fixed and permanent character that is only revealed, but not shaped by time. 'Human nature,' writes Middleton characteristically, 'has ever been the same in all ages and nations'.[38] In this, Middleton's sources, Livy and Dionysius Halicarnassus agreed, and helped to mislead him. Middleton defends the authority of Dionysius in particular, unmoved or perhaps unaware of the controversy then raging in France about 'the uncertainty of early Roman history'. Neither he nor anyone else in his time (with the one exception of that eccentric Neapolitan, Giambattista Vico) was prepared to anticipate Niebuhr and the 19th century.

As it turned out, however, it was not Middleton's use of Dionysius but his reliance on Cicero that proved him vulnerable. In 1742, a fellow Cambridge tutor, James Tunstall, launched the first unexpected blow against the letters of Brutus and Cicero, and the battle was joined.

Middleton was certainly taken aback. It is true that his personal relationship with Tunstall had been recently strained over a university election in which he failed to back his colleague, and that Tunstall had more conservative views of both religion and politics.[39] That he should find fault with Middleton's panegyric was perhaps to be expected, although the assault on the letters was a surprise. For several centuries, since their discovery by Petrarch, they had been pretty much accepted as authentic, though occasional doubts had been expressed. Middleton was certainly on guard against errors of this kind, and he noticed and rejected at least one forgery among his sources, the pseudo-Ciceronian *Consolatio*, and silently passed over several others, including the famous *Commentariolum Petitionis*, or as it was known in English translation, *The Art of Canvassing at Elections*, though both had advocates in his day.[40]

According to Charles Yorke, Tunstall tried to be tactful in his criticism. 'I was informed a few days ago,' he wrote to his brother, 'that Tunstall of St Johns is writing some observations on Dr Middleton's life of Cicero. He has in a very genteel way acquainted the Doctor with his Intentions, and has asked leave to address them to himself. It will give the Doctor room to explain himself in some points, and to correct in others.' Yorke thought that Tunstall was an able Ciceronian but feared that his criticism might carry him 'sometimes too far'.[41] It is very likely that Tunstall was inspired by a passage in the works of Erasmus, where that famous humanist had joined the suspicious letters of Phalaris with those of Seneca and Paul, and those of Brutus and Cicero, 'as the declamatory compositions of some sophist' (*declamatiunculae*).[42] This certainly is the argument of the Latin *Epistola ad Middleton* that Tunstall gave to the world in 1741, where he applies something of Bentley's technique to the task at hand. Tunstall argued there that the epistles gave themselves away as school compositions by their style, which was academic and lifeless, and by the fact that both correspondents wrote in essentially the same manner. On closer inspection, he found absurdities in sense, improprieties in language, suspicious predictions of future events, and many new historical facts that contradicted the genuine works of Cicero. Typically, the forger had carelessly introduced many errors of time and place and language which contradicted the dates, events, and style of the true letters. Tunstall recalled that the Greek, Plutarch, had quoted from this correspondence and he thought that it must have been this hint that had inspired the sophist to invent the missing documents.[43]

Middleton was exasperated by what he took to be Tunstall's 'ill nature and ill manners'. 'But it is my comfort,' he wrote to Lord Townshend, 'to find his performance to be an obscure, trifling, captious piece of Sophistry, what it is in my power to expose, as completely as I could wish.'[44] He did not think it would be worthwhile replying to the charge of bias; the only point that might be of interest to the learned world was the authenticity of the letters. He told Charles Yorke that he would vindicate their authority as materials, 'essential to Tully's life,' and that he meant to make his reply to Tunstall into a book, by translating them all.[45] The young man's reply to this information is interesting indeed, for only a year or two before, he and his brother, Philip, had themselves invented, with the help of a family friend, Thomas Birch, and some others, a series of imaginary letters purporting to be by a Persian emissary residing at Athens during the Peloponnesian War. These they published privately at just about this time (1741–43) in a limited edition of twelve copies, but when they reappeared in 1781, they were very much admired.[46] Charles, who was still in residence at Cambridge, had followed the whole Brutus affair with great interest, reporting events to his brother and the Athenian 'committee' in scrupulous detail. Meanwhile, Philip was having some fun of his own, concocting some obviously fictitious newsletters from the time of the Spanish Armada, only to have *them* pass for genuine afterwards, until they were finally exposed in 1839![47] It is intriguing to discover just what these forgers made of the alleged Ciceronian forgeries – to have as it were an expert's opinion; for it is clear that Charles and his friends spent much time and a good deal of effort making the pretended Athenian letters seem plausible and consistent, historically accurate and true to the sources, though they (like so many of the ancient sophists) had no desire to deceive anyone.[48]

In the early spring of 1742, Charles set down his own thoughts about the quarrel in a long letter to his brother and the committee. Although he apologized for the haste with which he had written out his 'rough minutes', it is evident that he had taken much pains over them and was proud of the little 'volume' that resulted.[49] He certainly wanted it to circulate and sent a copy to his old tutor, Henry Newcome, and much of the contents to William Warburton, though he had no wish to publish it or to offend either of the combatants. His letter, like his other contributions to the Athenian committee, seems to have been meant largely for his own education, and it was left to lie among the Hardwicke papers at Wimpole pretty much forgotten, until its recent transfer to the British Library.[50]

The little tract begins with a nod to Tunstall, who is commended for clearing up many doubtful passages in Cicero's letters and furnishing many helpful details about his life. Nevertheless, Yorke thought that the *Epistola* had been written too concisely to find a general audience, and that its many shrewd remarks were mixed with others either laboured or wrong. In particular, he agreed with his brother that the arguments against the Brutus-Cicero correspondence were mistaken ('rather a proof of acuteness than judgment'), and he tries to refute them one by one. He found the historical arguments unconvincing, because they could each be met by opposing probability to probability; and the linguistic arguments inadequate, because a modern understanding of ancient Latin usage was too precarious. To refute the letters, it was necessary to furnish contradictions, 'not obscure and dubious citations ingeniously wrested or mistaken'. To confirm their authenticity, it was necessary to devise conjectures, 'wherever they will enlighten what is dark, reconcile what is inconsistent, and supply what is wanting'. Even so, it was in the nature of letter-writing – particularly when a correspondence was broken or imperfect – that much should remain inexplicable and contradictory. Indeed, a competent sophist was not likely to leave it so; he 'would have been studiously exact in framing one letter with another, and rather attentive to the elegance and spirit of his compositions, than to give them the air of business, nature, and real life'.

It was up to Yorke, then, to furnish conjectures that might explain away the mistakes and inconsistencies in the letters, even while allowing that Cicero was not always consistent when circumstances were so swiftly changing. So, he set out to show that the dates of the letters might be mistaken because of scribal errors – Roman numerals depending often on a single stroke; that the prophecies in the letters were no more improbable than mere prudence would suggest, which (as Nepos says) *is* a sort of divination; that the contradictions with Plutarch were more likely due to Plutarch's unreliability than to a sophist's invention; and that various inconsistencies in substance could be reconciled by skilful and sympathetic interpretation of the texts. As for style, Yorke argues that Cicero's letters were not like his orations and hard to distinguish from other contemporary letters; that he wrote to Brutus with a reserve unlike his relationship with Atticus; and that while there were many 'hard and unique' expressions in the letters, we can no longer judge whether they were once permissible.[51] He was unable to find a single phrase, however peculiar, that was 'inconsistent with the Analogy of the Latin language'. In short, Yorke was satisfied that almost all the difficulties in the letters that Tunstall had found could either be emended or explained away. If the letters were spurious, he pointed out to Birch, they had led to great errors in the characters of Cicero and Brutus and their times; if genuine, they were inestimable monuments of antiquity, 'and in truth we have not so many ancient monuments transmitted to us that we can afford to lose any which are esteemed such'.[52]

It was a virtuoso performance for a young man and might well have gained him a literary reputation. But Charles Yorke, like his father, was more interested in high legal office, and so it was left to Middleton to make a public reply. In May 1742, he had already prepared a rebuttal; by September it was in the press. Yorke was pleased to hear that it was under way, 'since the learned world is extreamly interested in the question'. He was sure the Doctor would prove himself 'an old practiced disputant; he has certainly found out the weak places of a Town for the most part well fortified'.[53] As promised, Middleton's book was a complete translation of the letters with a Latin text and notes and a preface vindicating their genuine character.[54]

Apparently, Middleton never read Yorke's little piece, but his confidence was bolstered sufficiently by the general agreement of the scholarly world. He began his new work with a review of the literature from Petrarch's time, with a full list of the many famous scholars and editors who had accepted the letters as genuine. He does concede, however, that of the original eight books only eighteen letters of one of them had survived, until a few more were added by a German editor early in the 16th century. 'Though the novelty of the discovery surprised Critics a while, and made them cautious', they had come to be universally accepted.[55] If Tunstall was willing to condemn them all without distinction, Middleton was as ready to defend them all without qualification.

One trouble with Tunstall's argument was that he had provided neither forger, nor plausible motive for the forgery. If the forger had concocted these missives to complete the story recounted in the letters to Atticus, why had he left only a few unconnected epistles and fragments? And if he had meant to vindicate Cicero's character from the charge of favouring Octavian (the only answer, according to Middleton, that Tunstall would give him in conversation)[56], who was the sophist defending him against? After all, it was these very letters that had made the charge in the first place, so that the forger would have to be defending himself against himself, or at the least, Tunstall would have to invent two sophists. Middleton doubted that anyone in the Middle Ages had the skill to concoct such capable letters, or that anyone after Petrarch would have dared to put anything into the letters not expressly drawn from Cicero.

The reply to Tunstall's other charges was not more difficult and sounds a little like Charles Yorke. There was no point, Middleton argued, using Plutarch against the letter, because Plutarch was a notoriously unreliable source and a few contradictions could be easily explained. As for discrepancies with Cicero's other letters, it was easy to show how shifting circumstances could produce different sentiments. Middleton's Cicero was not an unwavering ideologue but a practical politician addressing different correspondents under the pressure of events. The dates of the letters were, it is true, sometimes discordant with events, but that was a notorious fault of scribes and could easily be adjusted. Finally, with regard to style, Middleton tried to show that there was indeed a difference between the two correspondents, but that such arguments were generally fruitless. 'All arguments from stile, are of too loose and precarious a nature, to have any great weight in questions of this sort; there being no settled rule or criterion to which we can apply them, but the different tast and judgment of different men.'[57] To show anachronistic language would be one thing (as Bentley had done with Phalaris); it was quite another to rule out small discrepancies of usage – unless one pretended to an absolute mastery of Latin, now impossible when so much ancient literature was lost. Tunstall had found the letters lifeless and futile, while Middleton thought them models of expression. On only one point perhaps were the two agreed: the epistle of Cicero to Octavian, which usually appeared with this correspondence, was undoubtedly a forgery, though Tunstall found it *similar* enough to the Brutus letters to prove that they too must be false, while Middleton thought it sufficiently *different* to proclaim their authenticity.[58]

When Middleton's book appeared, it must have seemed to everyone, as it first seemed to Warburton, that he had won the quarrel and settled the issues. But Tunstall was undeterred, exasperated rather than dismayed, and ready to reply. At the same time, another and a better scholar, Jeremiah Markland, was also pondering the question and getting ready to engage. It seemed to Warburton that there was bound to be a 'bloody fight' – and so it transpired.[59]

Publishers and readers in the 18th century seem to have had an extraordinary appetite for scholarly controversies of an abstruse and technical kind. Tunstall and Markland each produced big books full of minute argument, unleavened by either the wit or sarcasm of a Bentley or Boyle. Their only concession to popular taste was to write, like Bentley, in English, but they and Middleton were read for a long time in England and abroad and generated much further discussion. The fact is that the appetite for the classics was insatiable in a neo-classical age, and something important seemed to be at stake. As Tunstall put it, no doubt thinking of Bentley, 'The distinguishing of what is genuine and what is spurious, in the several writings which have come down to us under antient and celebrated names, is justly allowed the first place in the province of Criticism.' Without it, neither good history, nor good literature, was possible.[60]

Together, Tunstall and Markland divided the field. Although Tunstall said that it was the style and language of the letters that had first aroused his suspicions, he concentrated his own rebuttal on the discrepancies of sense which he thought Middleton had either missed or avoided. He even added an appendix at the back, by another old foe of Middleton's, John Chapman, to show that the letters (and Middleton) had gone astray in misnumbering the Roman legions.[61] Line by line, Tunstall defended his *Epistola*, mostly reiterating but occasionally adding to its arguments. Since Middleton had disputed Plutarch's authority, it was now necessary to defend it. Since Middleton had tried to adjust the dates of the letters to the facts, it was now necessary to point out the circularity of his argument. 'Reducing the dates to conformity with the facts is doubly begging the question; in proving the reality of the facts from the supposed genuineness of the Letters, and in answering objections to the Letters by supposing the reality of the facts.'[62] What is more, such *légerdemain* made it impossible for Tunstall to prove that the forecasts of events in the letters had been made after the fact through the hindsight of the forger.

Tunstall ends his long argument with some fresh remarks on the form and style of the letters, so unequal to the 'living imagery and figurative splendor,' of the rest of Cicero's writings.[63]

Who then was the forger? Middleton had denied flatly that there was anyone in the Middle Ages who was competent to invent such a remarkable work. Tunstall continued to believe in the possibility and suggested that fame, money or mistaken identity might well conjure up plausible Ciceronian inventions at any time. Even Middleton allowed that some frauds had deceived great men, like the letter of Cicero to Octavian that so resembled the suspected Brutus correspondence and had fooled Erasmus; or the fake *Consolatio* that Middleton so admired and seemed to Tunstall to surpass anything in the questionable letters. But the ancient world had already been full of forgeries, like the sophistic declamations described by Bentley; or the polished inventions of the pseudo-Sallust that misled Quintilian; or plain misattributions, like the *Rhetorica ad Herennium* which had mistakenly been fathered on Cicero, until recent scholarship reassigned it.[64] Even more to the point. were the various orations that had been falsely ascribed to the great orator, like the one, still surviving, 'which pretends to be spoken by him before he went into banishment'; or another, known only by title, that had recently appeared in a collection of Ciceronian fragments; or those anciently assigned to Antony and Catiline, but forged to detract from Cicero's character. There was even a fifth Catilinarian oration to add to the genuine ones.[65] Perhaps most to the point, were the many forged epistles, including several that had become attached to Brutus and Cicero. Apparently, there had once existed a whole fake correspondence between Cicero and a philosophical lady named Caerellia, not to mention the Greek letters of Brutus that had been answered by a sophist named Mithridates. Tunstall also remembers many imperial imitators of Cicero.[66]

In short, there was good reason to believe that the letters could have been forged in or near Cicero's own time. That this would make their exposure more difficult by reducing the chance of anachronism, and that it might also increase their historical value as contemporary testimony, does not seem to have bothered Tunstall. His main contention had been to show that there were important historical discrepancies between the suspected letters and the genuine ones, and to show therefore that the letters were a fraud contrived to bolster Cicero's reputation.[67] He was less interested in the forger, and it is one of the weaknesses of his argument that he never quite seems to have made up his mind about either the time or the purpose of the forgery.

Nevertheless, Markland thought that Tunstall had an unanswerable case. He had all along been scribbling critical notes in the margins of Middleton's translation, like a good student of Bentley's, and he thought that there was a lot more that could be said about the faulty language of the fake epistles. On that matter, indeed, even Tunstall needed some corrrection.[68] Markland was an excellent scholar in Latin and Greek, who had made many contributions to the criticism of classical authors, particularly to Horace, Statius, and Lysias, with Euripides still to come. He was the only one in his generation who could hope to aspire to the mantle of Bentley, whom he admired very much and used to visit frequently in old age. But he was an unworldly man with a somewhat narrow view of classical letters, a bit of a pedant without the stomach for real controversy. Twice, he was urged to run for Greek Professor at Cambridge, and twice he refused, retiring abruptly to the country to nurse his own modest wish to be left alone to pursue his favourite occupations, 'collating the Classical Authors of Antiquity or illuminating the Book of Revelation'.[69] 'He is a scholar undoubtedly,' said Dr Johnson impatiently, 'but remember that he would run from the world, and that it is not the world's business to run after him'.[70]

In 1745, at the prompting of his friend, the printer William Bowyer, he published his *Remarks on the Epistles of Cicero to Brutus and Brutus to Cicero*. The book was divided into three unequal parts: a consideration of the language of the letters, of their facts, and of their arguments, by which he intended to show their 'Bad Latin, False History and Bad Reasoning.'[71] In the end, he devoted most of his labour to the first part, where he showed how much in the letters failed to meet the standard of true Ciceronian Latin. Already, in his edition of Statius (1728), Markland had shown his skill and independence in these matters, defending in his preface the Bentleian prerogative of emending errors by conjecture against the dead weight of tradition. He believed that he had corrected almost 500 errors there and his work still has the respect of modern scholars.[72] Now, Markland was ready to show the suspected letters faulty, for their bad grammar, inadequate vocabulary, and their 'great Ignorance in the Propriety and Signification of the Latin Tongue'. Among other things, he discovered in them words not found elsewhere and altogether contrary to Latin etymology. This time, the *errores* were beyond correction, the result, he insisted, not of mistakes in the transmission of the text, but of outright forgery. Even so, Markland had to admit that the inventor, whoever he was, was a 'Person of quick Parts and Ingenuity, and of a share of Learning not very common in the Age in which he lived'. And he believed that the forgery must have been committed not long after Cicero's time.[73]

There is no denying Markland's learning or dexterity as he made his way through the little clues that were the grist to his mill. But Markland himself saw a problem in his method, in the limitations set by a dead language, imperfectly known. How was one to tell what correct usage was – what Cicero, for example, might have said on a given occasion – apart from what actually remained? 'We cannot now stir a step, nor join Two Words together so as to be secure from error, unless we have a precedent from the Writings of the Antients.' If Cicero were alive today, he would find innumerable mistakes in our Latin, just as we do with a Frenchman who composed in English only from a knowledge of books. We are bound, then, to demand an authority for every doubtful word or expression, though we can never be quite certain whether we know enough Latin to judge.

The best we can hope to do is to saturate ourselves in the language of the author. In this case, the result was obvious. 'If the frequent and attentive Reading of any Author's Works will enable a man (as it certainly will) to arrive at some degree of Discernment between the Writings of that Author and those of Another; I do not doubt but that any person who is conversant in Cicero's Works, and reads them with some Tast and Pleasure . . . would very soon perceive, that soever they are . . . [they] cannot be Cicero's.'[74]

It was almost inevitable that Markland should try out this same reasoning on some other works in the Ciceronian canon, and find them wanting also. In particular, he hit upon the four orations, *Post reditum*, as suspicious, and he immediately trained his criticism upon them. Any unprejudiced reader, he was sure, must agree that they 'were such silly and unnatural stuff,' that even a schoolboy would now be ashamed to write them. The fact that all the great scholars of the past had accepted them 'uncensur'd' did not ruffle him. Reason, not authority, was the only judge in these matters. 'For Good Sense and True Eloquence being much the same at all Times and in all Places, Mankind at present are surely in some manner Judges of these, tho' perhaps not as competent ones as the Antients were.'[75] A little later, Markland began to find some suspicious-looking passages even in the *De Oratore*.[76]

Still, Markland could never attain Bentley's confidence. 'Nothing is so common,' he saw, 'than for a Man of Letters to pronounce concerning Latin Expressions as Faulty, which have been proved afterwards from undoubted Authorities to be otherwise'.[77] At best, the philological arguments were meant only for the privileged few who could follow them, although they were the necessary groundwork for all higher culture. Markland had to be coaxed into finishing his work. What was required for complete conviction was the evidence of the historical contradictions and weak arguments in the letters and speeches. But here, Markland was content to refer to the work of his friend, Tunstall, and add only a few further examples. His long book concludes a little lamely, but he was quite sure that taken together, the arguments of the two friends were irrefutable.

For the moment philology faltered and the argument took another tack. To some it seemed that Middleton had been let off too easily in his reconstruction of Cicero's life. The actor and playwright, Colley Cibber, tried to restore the balance with his *Character and Conduct of Cicero Considered from the History of the Life of the Reverend Dr Middleton*, published early in 1747. Cibber offered no new evidence, only a more critical evaluation of Cicero's personality and politics. His work did little to advance the argument. The poet Gray wrote to Horace Walpole, complaining of 'whole Pages of Common-Place Stuff'. 'It is true,' he continued, 'he is often in the right with regard to Tully's Weaknesses, but was there any who did not see them?' Yet the problem of Middleton's bias was not so easily dismissed – or resolved.[78]

More mischievously, another young Cambridge student, John Ross, saw an opportunity in the fracas to have some fun. Like many who read Markland, he found the philological feuding a little futile, and he turned to the ever popular Augustan device of satire (perhaps assisted by Gray), to make his point.[79] In adding the orations to the letters, Markland had gone too far; but rather than attempt to meet him on his own ground, Ross thought to cast doubt on Markland's procedures by applying them even more outrageously to the rest of Cicero.

A Dissertation in which the Defence of Sulla ascribed to M. Tullius Cicero is proved to be Spurious, appeared anonymously in 1746, 'after the Manner of Mr Markland: with some Introductory Remarks on other Writings of the Antients never before Suspected'. The author begins with a homage to Markland for setting an example that could now be extended to many other Ciceronian works, as well as to Thucydides (some of whose history was obviously the work of an Alexandrian scribe), and even to some moderns also. There were, for example, a few sermons by Tillotson and Atterbury, 'so full of false English, weak Reasoning and Contradictions to the genuine Works, that it is impossible to suppose they could ever have been written by those venerable Prelates'.[80] The purpose of criticism was to free classical authors from charges of weakness, ignorance and error, introduced by forging sophists and declaimers. How nice it would be to reduce the number of such works for future editors and biographers! Though some would declare this scepticism dangerous to learning, in fact, freedom of judgement and the rules of criticism were in reality its best support.

The problem for the critic was thus to discover examples of bad language, false history, or bad reasoning, by which to convict the forger, since it must be assumed of great authors, 'that in whatever Piece these Marks are found, it could never be written by them'. If anyone disagreed, they would have to accept the epistles of Phalaris, of Brutus and Cicero, and the orations of Sallust to be genuine. Ross hoped that everyone would see that the ancients in general, and above all Cicero, 'could produce nothing but what was perfect in kind'. Emendation was always possible as a device for rescuing the classics, but substituting a word or phrase here and there made it impossible ever to condemn a work as spurious, 'and all Arguments founded upon internal Evidence would easily be avoided'. Better simply to discard the faulty piece altogether. Admit these assumptions, the rest was easy, and Ross's close parody of Markland follows. Cicero's defence of Sulla is shown to be 'a Confusion of Blunders, void of all Majesty, Dignity and Accuracy of Composition, so peculiar to the true History, and betraying an Ignorance in those Parts of History, with which he could not but be perfectly acquainted'.[81]

When Gray read the little work, he thought that Markland had been answered ingeniously, though he was worried that the irony was not quite 'transparent'.[82] Ross was surprised to discover, much later, that his tract could actually be read as a serious piece of criticism. He admitted writing the pamphlet and protested that 'It was intended to *laugh* at Mr Markland, and not, as you write, to *serve* him. The arguments, though flimsy and puerile, were his; and applied to writings undoubtedly genuine, in order to shew their insufficiency for the purpose to which he had applied them.'[83] But he was a little embarassed by his youthful trick. He was so far from decrying the methods of modern philology that he had really meant to support them (at least indirectly) by showing how they had been abused by Markland. A couple of years later, Ross brought out his own edition of Cicero's *Familiar Letters*, with a learned historical commentary and much praise for Middleton's *Cicero*. He hoped there, as a good scholar, to improve an understanding of the past, by building upon what had gone before, and even Markland, who found much fault with it, had to admit that he would probably win great reputation by it.[84]

Although Ross's parody did not end the quarrel nor settle any of the issues, the original combatants all lost heart or found other things to do. Middleton, who might otherwise have been expected to do battle, got embroiled in a new and larger controversy, this time over religious forgeries and the early Christian miracles, and altogether lost that peaceful repose that he pretended to desire.[85] Tunstall had tried twice already and had nothing left to say, though many years later he was still working on an edition of Cicero's letters to Atticus.[86] Markland withdrew abruptly from the field, scribbling over the title page of a copy of Ross, 'April 4, 1745, I never looked into this book', and leaving it to his friend, Bowyer, to write a feeble rejoinder in which he tried to meet satire with satire. A later generation continued to hold views on the matter, but it was left to the Germans, the new masters of classical philology, to take up the subject and make it their own.[87]

Just what they did about it is another and a longer tale that I shall not pretend to tell. Suffice it to say that the quarrel, which had started out in a university but found a general audience, ended up in the universities without anybody much noticing. The retreat of the classics in the 19th century is an old story which the decline in Cicero's public reputation nicely illustrates. But it is clear already in Markland, who spent his last days lamenting the decline of classical letters,[88] and clearer still in F.A. Wolf and his German successors, that the decline was due in part to the very advance that classical scholarship was making from generation to generation.[89] William Wotton had claimed that the modern classical scholar could come to know more than the ancients did about themselves. His enemies, and the coterie who attacked Bentley, were already frightened by the demands of a technical scholarship that was beyond their compass and their patience, and would like to have laughed the whole enterprise away. What neither Wotton nor his adversaries, nor Middleton and his, yet understood was that too much knowledge of antiquity was a dangerous thing; that the precise accumulation of detail, and the nice distinctions of authenticity, were bound to disclose, in the end, an antiquity far less familiar and less congenial to the present than the one that was taught in the schools and emulated in the world. From a practical point of view, the half-knowledge of a Temple or Swift, or for that matter, Charles Yorke and Conyers Middleton, was a better incentive to admire and employ the works of antiquity than the more profound scholarship of Bentley and Markland. In some ways, as Gaston Boissier noticed long ago, 'The man of the world is really more fitted to read the letters of Cicero than the German professor'.[90]

But I must not forget to tell you who did write the letters of Brutus and Cicero. According to the best modern opinion, the letters are indeed genuine, though one and perhaps two, still look a little suspicious.[91] And the orations too are authentic, though full of passages, to quote the Loeb Library editor, 'which are turgid, declamatory and vapid... Inaccuracies, forced antitheses and wearisome repititions are common; and the tone is often one of puerile swagger and malignity'.[92] Apparently, Cicero, like Homer, can sometimes be found to nod; and a standard of literary excellence, however persuasive, cannot by itself establish authenticity. Perhaps we may conclude by calling the old quarrel a draw; for there was something clearly to be said on both sides, and it took more than a century of further wrangling and careful inspection to sort things out. Nor is it impossible to imagine reopening the question one day, though for the time being we should no doubt be content to leave it to the experts.

References

1. It was conducted first in the Academie des Inscriptions et Belles-Lettres and printed in the *Memoires de littérature*; an English version was printed in the *Philological Miscellany* (London, 1761), p.87ff. A witness was Henry St John, Viscount Bolingbroke, who corresponded with one of the participants, Levèsque de Pouilly (*c.*1720), and whose *Letters on the Study and Use of History* (1735–38, published London, 1752) reflects the contest; see Bolingboke's *Works*, 4 vols. (Philadelphia, 1841), II, p.173ff.; 462ff. See also Louis de Beaufort, *Dissertation sur l'incertitude des cinq premières siècles de l'histoire romaine* (Utrecht, 1738); translated into English in 1740.
2. See the article 'Hardouin' in Jaques George de Chaufepié, *Nouveau dictionnaire historique et critique* (Amsterdam, 1750), II; and the biography by Charles-Etienne Jordan of Hardouin's great enemy, Mathurin de la Croze, *Histoire de la vie et des oeuvres de M. de la Croze* (Amsterdam, 1741), p.79ff. In England, John Chapman detected a dangerous Jesuit plot; popularized the controversy in several tracts; and was answered by Middleton in his *Free Inquiry* (1748) (see below). William Bowyer printed a manuscript by Hardouin as late as 1766 with remarks by Caesar de Missy,. reviewing the arguments, *Ad censuram scriptorum veterum prolegomena*; see William Bowyer, *Miscellaneous Tracts*, ed John Nichols (London, 1785), pp.478–82; *Biographical and Literary*

Anecdotes of William Bowyer, ed. John Nichols (London, 1782), pp.367–68.

3. For the Trojans, see Jacob Perizonius's dissertation, in *Dictys Cretensis et Dares de bello et excidio Trojae* (Amsterdam, 1702); for Annius, see E. Tigerstedt, 'Ioannis Annius and Graeca Mendax', *Classical, Medieval and Renaissance Studies in Honor of B.L. Ullman* (Rome, 1964, II, p.293ff.; C.R. Ligotta, 'Annius of Viterbo and the Historical Method', *Journal of the Warburg and Courtauld Institutes*, 50 (1987), pp.44–56.
4. For example, Jeremiah Jones, *A New and Full Method of Settling the Canonical Authority of the New Testament*, 2 vols. (London, 1726), which prints and discusses many of the suspicious texts; see also, Lenglet du Fresnoy, 'Rules for the Discovery of Spurious Works', *A New Method for Studying History*, trans. Richard Rawlinson, 2 vols. (London, 1728), I, pp.304–15.
5. Ch.27, 'Of the Philological Learning of the Moderns', *Reflections upon Ancient and Modern Learning*, (London, 1694), pp.310–21.
6. Ibid., p.319.
7. Bentley's 'Dissertation upon the Epistles of Phalaris, Themistocles, Socrates, Euripides, etc., and Aesop's Fables', in Wotton's *Reflections*, 2nd ed. (London, 1697), p.62. The new work was entitled *A Dissertation upon the Epistles of Phalaris* (London, 1699). It has been reprinted with notes and the annexed dissertations of 1697 by Wilhelm Wagner (London, 1883). 'Boyle's' rejoinder was entitled *Dr Bentley's Dissertations on the Epistles of Phalaris... Examined* (London, 1698). A good account, indispensable for all things Bentleian, remains James Henry Monk, *The Life of Richard Bentley*, 2 vols (London, 1833), I, pp.78–138. I have written about the quarrel in: 'Ancients and Moderns Reconsidered', *Eighteenth Century Studies*, 15 (1981–82) pp.72–89; 'The Battle of the Books and the Shield of Achilles', *Eighteenth Century Life*, 9 (1984), pp.33–61; and 'Ancients, Moderns and History', *Humanism and History* (Ithaca, 1987), pp.155–77.
8. Bentley, *Dissertation* (1697), p.9.
9. Brutus's Greek epistles with a Latin translation by T. Naogeorgus (1558) were later coupled with the epistles of Phalaris (Heidelberg, 1597); there is a modern edition by Luigi Torraca (Naples, 1971).
10. For the Pseudo-Petronius, see J.A. Farrer, *Literary Forgeries* (London, 1907), pp.13–21; it was translated into English in 1694 and 1708; for the Cicero, see Evan T. Sage, *The Pseudo-Ciceronian Consolation (Chicago, 1910)*. According to Thomas Hearne, the *Consolatio* had been exposed in the 16th century, 'and is now known to every one to be a spurious Piece,' though Gilbert Burnet for one still thought otherwise, 'being ignorant of the matter and having no Judgment, or but very little in Tully's Style,' *Remarks and Collections*, ed. C.E. Doble et al., 11 vols. (Oxford, 1885–1921), I, p.154. Carlo Inghirami's *Etruscarum antiquitatum fragmenta* was published at Frankfort, 1637.
11. *Perfrictae frontis, aut judicii imminuti*; see Monk, I, 52–4.
12. Bentley, *Dissertation* (1697), p.134. For comparable modern discussions, see Franz Susemihl, *Geschichte der Grieschischen Litteratur in der Alexandrinerzeit*, 2 vols. (Leipzig, 1892), I, pp.597–601, 634–39, 652; Alfred Gudeman, 'Literary Frauds among the

Greeks', *Classical Studies in Honor of Henry Drisler*, (New York, 1894), pp.52–74. The fullest recent account of ancient forgeries would seem to be Wolfgang Speyer, *Die literarische Fälschung im Heidnischen und Christlichen Altertum* (Munich, 1971).

13. See Joseph M. Levine, 'Bentley's Milton: Philology and Criticism in Eighteenth Century England', forthcoming in the *Journal of the History of Ideas*.
14. Middleton, *Works*, 4 vols. (London, 1751), II, p.417. I have made good use of the manuscript biography by M.L. Clarke on deposit in Trinity College Library, Cambridge. There is useful Middleton correspondence in the Sussex County Record Office, The British Library and Trinity College. See also Dorothy M. Stuart, 'Some Unpublished Letters of John Lord Hervey and Dr Conyers Middleton', *English*, 2 (1938), pp.7–18.
15. See Middleton, *Works*, ii, 350; and Horace Walpole's anecdotes relating to Middleton in the *Correspondence*, ed. W.S. Lewis et al., vol.15 (New Haven, 1952), app.1. Middleton shared his musical tastes with Harley; see the correspondence in the Portland Papers, B. Loan 29/167.
16. See Monk, II, 38ff.
17. Middleton to Hervey, August 18, 1734; B.L. Add. MS 32458, f.185; ibid., Sept. 15, 1733, B.L. Add. MS passim 5846, f.12v. There is good testimony to Middleton's personal piety from an unimpeachable source, the very conservative William Cole; see B.L. Add. MS5846, f.12.
18. Joseph Spence, *Observations, Anecdotes and Characters*, ed. James M. Osborn, 2 vols. (Oxford, 1966), I, pp.337–38. For Cicero's fortunes during the Enlightenment, see Th. Zielinski, *Cicero im Wandel der Jahrhunderte*, 3rd ed. (Leipzig, 1912), ch.16–17, a very incomplete account, however.
19. Middleton knew George Lyttelton's *Observations on the Life of Cicero* (London, 1733) and Jacques Morabin's *The History of Cicero's Banishment* (London, 1725), the English translation dedicated to Wharton. When Lyttleton read Middleton's life, he was filled with admiration and envied his choice of subject, 'the age of Cicero – that age which above all others, before or since, furnishes the noblest materials for history.' Lyttleton to Warburton, Oct. 7, 1737, William Warburton, *A Selection from Unpublished Papers*, ed. Francis Kilvert (London, 1841), pp.197–200.
20. Middleton to Hervey, Nov. 9, 1738, B.L. Add. MS32458, f.59.
21. Hervey to Middleton, Nov. 7, 1738, ibid., f.59.
22. Middleton to Hervey, Sept. 22, 1737, ibid., f.5.
23. *The History of the Life of Marcus Tullius Cicero*, 2 vols. (London, 1741). There were eight editions in England alone by 1767, with many more to follow, as well as translations into French, Spanish and Italian. I quote for convenience from the three-volume edition (standard after 1741), London, 1810. For the enthusiastic reception, see Henry Seymour Conway to Horace Walpole, Feb. 21, 1742, Walpole *Correspondence*, 37, pp.94–5; J. Hinckesman to Samuel Jebb, May 9, 1741, in Christopher Wordsworth, *Scholae Academicae* (Cambridge, 1877), pp.314–15. When Hervey read some of the manuscript to the Princess Caroline, she cried out that 'It was

the prettyest and most entertaining thing she had ever read in her life', Hervey to Middleton, Dec. 9, 1738, B.L. Add. MS32458, f.68.

24. Middleton to Warburton, Oct. 27, 1739, B.L. Add. MS32457, ff.143–44. Fielding's parody is in *An Apology for the Life of Mrs Shamela Andrews* (London, 1741); see the edition by Martin Battestin (Boston, 1961), pp.301–03, 367n; cf. *Joseph Andrews*, ibid., pp.201–02, 364n. 'Shamela and the Dedication to it,' reports Charles Yorke in 1741, 'The former as a ridicule on Pamela, and the latter on the Dedication to the life of Cicero, meet with general applause,' B.L. Add. MS35633, ff.31–2. In May, he adds that the flattering dedication, 'handsomely drawn up, draws a great deal of odium, and sneer, and censure on the Doctor,' ibid., ff.40–1.

25. 'That noted passage alone, of Tully in his second book of the Dialogues on Oratory, is more than enough to afford the necessary instructions for him who has the mind to play the Historian', Lenglet du Fresnoy, *A New Method of Studying History*, I, pp.x–xi. See Middleton, *Cicero*, I, pref., p.xix; III, sect. 12, pp.351–52. The *De Oratore* was translated twice in the period, by G.P. (London, 1723) and William Guthrie (London, 1742).

26. Ibid., III, sect. 12, p.346.

27. Ibid., I, pref., p.xxix.

28. Ibid., III, sect. 3, pp.253–54.

29. Ibid., II, sect. 6, pp.48–9.

30. Middleton to Warburton, Sept. 11, 1736, in [John Towne], *The Argument of the Divine Legation Stated* (London, 1751), pp.162–72; Middleton, *Cicero*, III, sect. 12, pp.395–400.

31. Mrs Donellan to Elizabeth Montagu, April 15, 1741, in Emily J. Climenson, *Elizabeth Montagu*, 2 vols. (London, 1906), I, pp.70–71. The Duchess of Portland was also reading Middleton that Spring and seemed to share these sentiments, ibid., p.82. Middleton tried to avoid what he called 'the natural prejudice of Biographers,' but even Hervey chided him for it; see Hervey to Middleton, Dec. 7, 1738, B.L. Add. MS32458, ff.66–7. See also Charles to Philip Yorke, B.L. Add. MS35633, ff.40–1; Daniel Wray to Philip Yorke, B.L. Add. MS35401, ff.3–4.

32. Middleton, *Cicero*, III, sect. 9, p.106; II, Sect. 7, pp.188–89; III, sect. 12, pp.374–92.

33. Ibid., I, p.6; cf. II, sect. 6, p.111. See Melvyn New, 'Gibbon, Middleton, and the "Barefooted Fryars"', *Notes and Queries*, 223 (1978), p.51–2; Levine, *Humanism and History*, pp.190–91.

34. Middleton, *Cicero*, II, sect. 11, p.285. For the special value of letters to history, see Lenglet du Fresnoy, *A New Method of History*, I, p.225.

35. Middleton, *Cicero*, II, sect. 11, pp.282–83; 302; II, sect. 9, pp.72–3.

36. Nicholas Hubert Mongault, *Lettres de Ciceron à Atticus avec des remarques* (Paris, 1714). Middleton credits several other previous writers in his preface but overlooks William Bellenden's massive Latin compilation, *De tribus luminibus Romanorum* (Paris, 1634), for which he was later accused unfairly of plagiarism; see M.L. Clarke, 'Conyers Middleton's Alleged Plagiarism', *Notes and Queries*, Feb. 1983, pp.44–6.

37. *A Treatise on the Roman Senate* (London, 1747). Thomas Gray, who was a friend, dimissed it in a letter to Wharton, as 'well enough, but nothing of great Consequence,' March 17, 1747, *Correspondence*, ed. Paget Toynebee and Leonard Whibley, 3 vols. (Oxford, 1935), I, pp.272–79. The controversy began with the Abbé Vertot and Earl Stanhope in 1721 and came to involve, besides Hervey and Middleton, Thomas Chapman, Nathaniel Hooke, Edward Spelman and William Bowyer. See also Edward Wortley Montagu, *Reflections on the Rise and Fall of the Antient Republicks adapted to the Present State of Great Britain* (London, 1759).
38. Middleton, *Cicero*, I, ded., p.ii; cf. *Works*, I, pp.186–87. For Collingwood, see the *Idea of History*, ed T.M. Knox (Oxford, 1946).
39. Middleton to Townshend, Oct. 29, 1741, Trinity College MS. R1.88, f.45; Middleton to Warburton, Oct. 22, 1741, Middleton, *Works*, II, pp.488–90.
40. Middleton, *Cicero*, II, sect. 8, p.402. The *Consolatio* was translated and defended by Thomas Bracklock in his *Paraclesis* (Edinburgh, 1767). The *Commentariolum petitionis* appeared anonymously as, *The Art of Canvassing at Elections, Perfect in all Respects and Highly Necessary to be understood by the Electors, no less than by the Candidates, written two thousand years ago, for one of the greatest scholars, and most consummate Statesmen then in the World* (London, 1714). Its authenticity as a contemporary work is still debated; see M.I. Henderson, '*De Commentariolo Petitionis*', *Journal of Roman Studies*, 40 (1950), pp.8–21; supported by W.S. Watt, ibid., n.s. 7 (1958), 32–44; and opposed by J.P.V.D. Balsdon, 'The *Commentariolum Petitionis*', *Classical Quarterly*, n.s. 13 (1963), 242–50. The Loeb editor, M. Cary, reviews the question and leaves it still open, *Letters to Brutus* (Cambridge, 1972), p.739.
41. Charles to Philip Yorke, June 2, 1741, B.L. Add. MS35360, ff.42–3. Tunstall's work was delayed in printing by the university election for orator, ibid., Oct. 13, 1741, ff.48–9.
42. Erasmus to Beatus Rhenanus, May 27, 1521, *Opus Epistolarus*, ed. P.S. Allen, 4 (Oxford, 1922), p.501. See Letizia A. Panizza, 'Gasparino Barzizza's Commentaries on Seneca's Letters', *Traditio*, 33 (1977) p.305ff.
43. Tunstall, *Epistola ad virum eruditorum Conyers Middleton* (Cambridge 1741), pp.192–253.
44. Middleton to Townshend, May 12, 1742, Trinity College MS. R 1. 88, f.47.
45. Charles Yorke to Thomas Birch, [May? 1742], B.L. Add. MS4325, ff.44–5.
46. *Athenian Letters or the Epistolary Correspondence of an Agent of the King of Persia residing at Athens during the Peloponnesian War*, 2 vols. (London, 1741–43). A manuscript with minutes of the committee for reviewing the letters (1741) and related materials can be found in B.L. Add. MS4326A; and there is correspondence relating to the project in B.L. Add. MS35360 and 35396 and elsewhere in the Hardwicke Papers. See Philip Yorke, *Life and Correspondence of Phillip Yorke, Earl of Hardwicke*, 3 vols. (Cambridge, 1913), I, pp.207–08; George Hardinge, *Biographical Anecdotes of Daniel Wray* (London, 1815), p.32ff.
47. *English Mercuries published by authority in Queen Elizabeth's . . . Time;* see Thomas Watts,

A Letter to Antonio Panizzi . . . on the Reputed Earliest Printed Newspaper (London, 1839); *Gentleman's Magazine*, 126 (1850) pt.i, pp.485–91.

48. See especially the letters in B.L. Add. MS35360 and Charles Yorke to Birch, Aug. 31, 1741, B.L. Add. MS35400, f.365.
49. Charles to Philip Yorke, B.L. Add. MS35633, f.79.
50. The *Athenian Letters* 'was begun and carried merely for our own Improvement and our own Entertainment, without any Intention of aiming at Reputation', Philip Yorke to Birch, Sept. 5, 1742. B.L. Add. MS35396, ff.54–5.
51. Arguments from taste and language, 'could not be used with much weight in the present question, except to a native of Rome, and a contemporary of Cicero,' Yorke to Warburton, B.L. Add. MS35404, ff.6–7.
52. Charles Yorke to Birch [May? 1742], B.L. Add. MS4325, ff.44–5.
53. Ibid., ff.44–5; and to Warburton, May 11, 1742, B.L. Add. MS35404, ff.8–9.
54. *The Epistles of Cicero to Brutus* (London, 1743). The letters are preceded by an introduction of 127 pages.
55. *Episltes*, pp.viii–ix. A. Cratander's edition (1528) is discussed in the preface to *Epistulae ad M. Brutum*, ed Lucianus Linaz (Milan, 1971), pp.27–40, with bibliography, pp.41–5.
56. *Epistles*, p.xviii. Middleton and Tunstall seem to have belonged to the same Cambridge club, the Old Maids, which met regularly at a coffee-house after evening chapel for literary conversation; see Christopher Wordsworth, *Social Life at the English Universities in the Eighteenth Century* (Cambridge, 1874), p.156.
57. *Epistles*, p.cxiv.
58. Ibid., pp.cxx–cxxii; Tunstall, *Epistola*, p.221. It was already suspected by Petrus Victorius (1536), see the *Epistola ad Octavianum*, ed. R. Lomacchia (Milan, 1967), pp.54–5.
59. Warburton to Birch, Jan. 18, 1743, *Illustrations of the Literary History of the Eighteenth Century*, ed. John Nichols, 8 vols. (London, 1817–58), II, p.129; Warburton to Middleton, Nov. 23, 1742, Walpole, *Correspondence*, 15, pp.10–11.
60. Tunstall, *Observations on the Present Collection of Epistles between Cicero and M. Brutus* (London, 1744) p.2; Bentley, *Dissertations* (Wagner ed.), p.78.
61. 'A Letter from Dr Chapman on the Antient Numerical Character of the Roman Legions' (April 19, 1744), Tunstall, *Observations*, pp.413–35.
62. Ibid., p.245.
63. Ibid., p.379.
64. See the edition by Harry Caplan (Cambridge, 1954); Victorius had already (1582) ascribed it to one Cornificius, as here; but Caplan leaves the authorship still uncertain. For the Pseudo-Sallust, see the discussion in Ronald Syme, 'The False Sallust', *Sallust* (Berkeley, 1964), app.II, pp.313–51; and the edition by A. Ernout (Paris, 1962).
65. Tunstall, *Observations*, p.49. For the spurious *Pridie quam in exilium iret,* challenged within a few years of its discovery by Petrarch, see *Texts and Transmissions: A Survey of*

the Latin Classics, ed. L.D. Reynolds (Oxford, 1983), p.75. Tunstall notes some other frauds ascribed to Plautus and Caesar, as well as the false letters between Sallust and Cicero, Seneca and Paul.

66. Cf. Alfred Gudeman, 'Literary Frauds among the Romans', *Transactions of the American Philological Society*, 25, 1894, pp.140–64; Evelyn H. Clift, *Latin Pseudepigrapha* (Baltimore, 1945).
67. Tunstall, *Observations*, pp.63, 177, 216ff. Tunstall grudgingly concedes to Middleton that there were no signs of later Latin in the letters, but he avoids the consequence by arguing that that might be due to the success of the sophist in gaining authenticity; ibid., pp.399–400.
68. Markland's copy of Middleton's *Epistles*, with his notes, is in the British Library; on p.21, he corrects Tunstall. See Markland to Bowyer, Sept. 20, 1744, Bowyer, *Miscellaneous Tracts*, pp.570–72.
69. *Literary Anecdotes*, IV, p.659; and the inscription on his tomb, ibid., 310; Markland announced his retirement on April 7, 1744; see *Anecdotes Biographical and Literary of the late William Bowyer*, ed. John Nichols (London, 1778), p.22n.; the reason was never made clear. There are appreciations of Markland's scholarship by Elmesly in the *Quarterly Review*, 7 (1812), pp.441–64 and recently by C. Collard in the *Cambridge Philological Society Transactions*, n.s., 22 (1976), pp.1–13. Housman placed him, with Porson, second only to Bentley among English classicists; *Classical Papers*, ed. J. Diggle and F.R.D. Goodyear (Cambridge, 1972), III, p.1005.
70. Hester Lynch Piozzi, *Anecdotes of the Late Samuel Johnson,* ed. Arthur Sherbo (London, 1974), p.143.
71. Markland, *Remarks*, p.7.
72. See J.A. Willis, 'The *Silvae* of Staius and their Editors', *Phoenix*, 20 (1966), pp.314–20; the preface to Statius is quoted in Collard, p.7. For contemporary praise, see Gottlieb Curtius to J.P. D'Orville, Oct. 1729, Bodl. MS. D'Orville 486, ff.110–11.
73. Markland, *Remarks*, pp.23, 232.
74. Ibid., pp.91, 224. Behind this comment there lies the whole long Ciceronian quarrel of the 16th century, still very much alive in the 18th. Erasmus's *Ciceronianus* was reprinted at Oxford as late as 1693; it is discussed in the biographies of Erasmus by Samuel Knight (Cambridge, 1726), pp. pp.200–1, and John Jortin (London, 1758), pp.443–53. In general, see Izora Scott, *Controversies over the Imitation of Cicero* (New York, 1910).
75. Markland, *Remarks*, pp.227, 230.
76. Markland to Bowyer, June 1749, *Literary Anecdotes*, IV, p.283. He also found many bad verses in the *Aeneid*, 'which he, though a bad poet, would not have suffered to appear in any composition of his own', ibid., 275.
77. Markland, *Remarks*, p.127.
78. Gray to Walpole, Feb. 1747, Gray, *Correspondence*, I, 264. Middleton's partiality continued to be questioned by subsequent writers, e.g. William Guthrie, *Cicero's Epistles to Atticus*, 2 vols. (London, 1752), I, pp.vi, 134; II, pp.439, 447; Nathaniel

Hooke, *The Roman History*, III (London, 1764), 321, 333, 373–79, etc.; VI (London, 1771), 208–10; William Melmoth, *Cicero's Letters to Several of His Friends*, 3 vols. (London, 1753), II, p.142n; III, pp.307n, 382–83n. The portrait in B.Y. Tyrrell and I.C. Purser, *The Correspondence of M. Tullius Cicero,* third ed., 7 vols. (1904–33) is, however, surprisingly close to Middleton's.

79. *Literary Anecdotes*, II, 184n.
80. Ross, *Dissertation*, p.5.
81. Ibid., pp.49–54.
82. From Gray's copy of Ross, quoted by Mitford in his edition of *The Correspondence of Thomas Gray and William Mason* (London, 1853), p.204n. The German, F.A. Wolf (see below), also seems to have missed the irony; see *Literary Anecdotes*, V, pp.412–13.
83. Ross to George Ashby, Oct. 4, 1780, *Literary Anecdotes*, II, p.186.
84. Cicero, *Epistolarum ad familiares*, ed. John Ross, 2 vols. (Cambridge, 1749); Markland to Bowyer, June 9 and 20, 1749, *Literary Anecdotes*, IV, pp.316–20.
85. According to Thomas Birch, the whole impression of Middleton's *Free Inquiry into the Miraculous Powers* (1748), 3,000 copies, was sold off in a single day! See Birch to Lord Orrery, Dec. 30, 1748, *The Orrery Papers*, ed. Countess of Cork and Orrery, 2 vols. (London, 1903), I, pp.48–50. There is a manuscript among Middleton's papers entitled, 'Remarks on the letter from Abgarus to Jesus, with the answer, together with the letters', B.L. Add. MS32459, ff.46–9v. The *Free Inquiry* was preceded, and the appetite of the audience whetted, by a *Preliminary Discourse*, a year earlier; the outcry was extraordinary. Middleton died in July, 1750.
86. Tunstall died in 1762, the letters still incomplete and unpublished; see Samuel Pegge, *Anonymiana*, (London, 1809), pp.177–78.
87. *Literary Anecdotes*, IV, p.281n. Bowyer's pamphlet (if he was the author) is entitled. *A Dissertation in which the Objections of a late Pamphlet . . . after the Manner of Mr Markland are clearly answered* (London, 1746); see *Literary Anecdotes*, II, pp.185–87. Bowyer tried to get Markland to edit all of Cicero's letters, to no avail; his notes on Middleton may be found in his *Miscellaneous Tracts*, ed. John Nichols (London, 1785), p.281ff.
88. Markland to Bowyer, April 11, 1763; *Literary Anecdotes*, IV, p.288.
89. F.A. Wolf, ed. *Orationes quattuor* (Berlin, 1801), answering J.M. Gesner who had opposed Markland in his *Cicero restitutus* (Göttingen, 1753–54). Wolf extended Markland's criticism to several other orations and for a time convinced Niebuhr. Eventually, the worm turned (several times) until a consensus finally emerged at the end of the 19th century. For an appreciation of Wolf, see Anthony Grafton, 'Prolegomena to Friedrich August Wolf', *Journal of the Warburg and Courtauld Institutes*, 44 (1981), pp.101–29.
90. Quoted approvingly by B.Y. Tyrrell and I.C Purser, *The Correspondence of Cicero*, I, pp.6–7. See Gaston Boissier, *Cicero and his Friends*, trans. A.D. Jones (New York, 1925), pp.19–21.

91. The suspicious letters are I, pp.16–17 (nos.17, 25 in the Loeb ed. where they are accepted as genuine; see M. Cary [1972], pp.618–19). See Tyrrell and Purser, VI, p.cix, with a good review of the whole controversy; D.R. Shackleton-Bailey, ed. *Correspondence of Cicero and Brutus* (Cambridge, 1980), pp.6–15.
92. N.H. Watts, *Cicero: The Speeches, Post Reditum, etc.* (Cambridge, 1935), pp.46–7. The second speech, *Ad Quirites*, was still being rejected in Teuffel's *History of Roman Literature*, revised by Ludwig Schwabe, trans. George C. Warr, 2 vols. (New York, 1892), p.290. In 1911, there was an attempt to indict the *Pro Murena* as a forgery by Poggio, but without success; see G.A. Harrer, 'The Genuineness of Cicero's *Pro Murena*', *Classical Philology*, 9 (1914), pp.83–4. Various false orations have been brought together in the Italian translation of Cicero's works, *Tutte le opere di Cicerone*, vol.33, ed Maria de Marco (Milan, 1967).

Forgery and the rise of the London Scriveners' Company

NIGEL RAMSAY

PROBLEMS of forgery were rife in medieval English society, and they were exacerbated as more reliance was placed on written documents for commercial transactions.[1] From the 12th century onwards, it was common to employ professional scribes as the writers of such instruments, and whether or not the parties who employed them or relied on their products were literate, it was inevitable that most instruments would have to be taken on trust.[2] In the absence of a fully-fledged notarial system in English commercial life, authenticity had to be ascertained from the instruments themselves, and given the shortcomings of practical diplomatic testing, it followed that much depended on the writers' honesty.[3] In this paper I shall be suggesting that the lack of any set of controls over professional scribes (such as that operated through the lawcourts in countries with a notarial system) combined with the prevalence of forgeries to result, in the 14th century, in the establishment of a professional organisation for the document-writers based in London. Monopolistic (within London), self-regulating, and regulated by the City's authorities, the London Scriveners' Company was to prosper on the back of the belief that its members could be trusted.

Most significant English documents in the medieval period were authenticated by bearing a seal, impressed on them *en placard* or, far more commonly, attached to them by a ribbon, cord, parchment or a strip of the document itself. Signatures made a brief appearance in this country after the arrival here of the Italian Lanfranc as Archbishop of Canterbury, and are occasionally found later, but the seal remained pre-eminent.[4] The authenticating signature, or at least the signature-by-itself, remained a southern European characteristic throughout the high middle ages, while in England use of the seal became increasingly widespread. As a pictorial device, the seal was easily recognizable by the illiterate, while it became accepted practice for people who lacked their own seal-matrix or seal-ring to use the seal of someone else.[5] Loss of a seal-matrix was a fearful calamity, and institutions took pains to guard against this or unauthorised use by keeping their seal under lock and key and preferably under several keys, different people each having one and all needing to come together to unlock it.[6]

The development of the counter-seal was another means that institutions and prominent ecclesiastical and lay magnates pioneered, to prevent their seal impressions being tampered with.[7] Seals were used in Anglo-Saxon England and yet there is nothing in the Anglo-Saxon laws that refers to forgery of them. But the 12th-century legal treatise known (after its supposed author) as *Glanvill* contains the statement that it is treasonable to forge the king's charters, just as it is treasonable to forge his coin.[8] The thinking that inspired Glanvill was the Roman law, which included within the crime of *maiestas* (*crimen lesae maiestatis* or *lèse-majesté*) the counterfeiting or destroying or desecrating or displaying lack of respect for the image of the emperor through making a fraudulent likeness of him.[9]

Most unfortunately for the development of English law, as we may think, throughout the middle ages and well into the Tudor period the English crime of forgery remained limited to the application, construction and slight extension of this principle – that it was only forgery if the king's seal was fraudulently imitated. Furthermore, it was not just any seal of the king's that had to be imitated: it was only his Great Seal and Privy Seal that counted for the common law, and it was these alone that were mentioned in the Statute of Treason passed in 1352.[10] The commonest method of forging a seal was by taking a genuine old one and applying it to the spurious document, and naturally the 1352 statute was construed to cover this practice.[11] Equally, it was not too difficult to regard a servant's forgery of his master's seal as a form of petty treason,[12] while within the Church a development of Roman law principles again led to a doctrine equivalent to treason that dealt with the forgery of papal bulls and other letters bearing the papal seal (or *bulla*).[13]

The defect in the common and statute laws was that no protection was offered to private individuals whose seal was being forged or misapplied.[14] For instance, as early as 1207 we find that when William de Frehorne repudiated a charter which was alleged to be his, saying that he had not made it or had it made, although he admitted that it bore the impression of his own seal, it was held that since he acknowledged his seal, he was bound by the charter.[15] The common law was uneasy about charters, especially when it was dealing with charters that purported to pass rights in land, and it preferred not to look into them too closely.[16] In 1371 there was a petition (or bill) in parliament that the forgery of private seals and their attachment to deeds should be punishable with life imprisonment, upon indictment – that it should in fact be made a felony – but this was rejected.[17] Only if its own records were involved did the Crown feel a duty to investigate and to punish; feet of fines and other essentially private instruments that had been brought before the king's Justices could thus achieve statutory protection.[18]

The Crown was occasionally ready to intervene, by issuing commissions for the arrest of forgers of, say, shrieval seals or of prominent ecclesiastics' seals,[19] but in general the only hope for private individuals who were the forger's victims was to petition the Chancellor to use his equitable jurisdiction on their behalf.[20] The only statutory remedy that was offered in the medieval period came in 1413, when it was enacted that if a title to real estate was disturbed or threatened by forged title deeds, then the guilty person should be fined.[21]

Henry VIII in 1536 extended the 1352 Statute of Treason's categories to cover forgery of the royal signet or sign manual – perhaps partly because of a recent instance of his sign manual being counterfeited by the keeper of his palace.[22] A Marian parliament in 1553 repeated the Henrician legislation, after William Hackney had forged a bill granting him 40 marks a year for life, signed 'Mary the Quene'. He was accordingly found guilty of high treason.[23] Help for the ordinary individual came only in 1563 when it was provided that forgers of evidences in regard to land, or those who offered such forged evidences in court, if they committed such a crime a second time, should be held as felons and forfeit the advantage of benefit of clergy.[24]

That is the short story of the common law. Let me turn now to the detection of forgeries. Palaeographical analysis was rarely applied, although one can point to occasional instances (mostly within monastic houses) of the forger's conscious imitation of archaic script and thus of an awareness of the changing forms of handwriting.[25] The seal was the hardest part of a document to imitate, and, as I have indicated, the commonest form of forgery was to transfer a genuine seal impression from one document to the false one. In the early 13th-century treatise known as *Bracton*, it is to the seal that the analysis of forgery turns first.[26] The forger's method was to slit the seal impression and transfer the two halves to the cords or strips of parchment of the spurious document; or to cut the cord, transfer the seal and cord, and seek to hide the join in the cord ends; otherwise, he might try to alter the handwriting on a genuine document. Other methods were possible, of course; the most sophisticated involved the officials of the institution whose document was to be forged. For instance, in 1607 the Chancery clerk George Leak, whose duty it was to engross the royal letters patent, took an ordinary piece of parchment on which he superimposed another of the same size but of an extraordinary thinness. He fastened the two sheets together at their margins with mouth-glue (sugar, water and glue), so that they appeared to be only one, and he passed the label or seal-tag through this double sheet. He then wrote a legitimate patent on the (uppermost) thin sheet, and had the Great Seal affixed to the label. Tag and seal were thus attached to the double sheet. He then had only to cut off the glued margin and remove the uppermost (inscribed) sheet, leaving himself with the blank sealed lower sheet. His handiwork would have been diplomatically faultless.[27]

A case comparable in its ingenuity is one that is well-known to palaeographers, thanks to its publication by J.F. Baldwin and L.C. Hector.[28] In 1432 John Lydeyard was prosecuting a claim to certain Oxfordshire manors against Thomas Seyntcler and others. Seyntcler's case depended in part on one ancient deed, while another document, an inquisition *post mortem*, was strong evidence against Lydeyard's case. This inquisition contained the statement that the deceased's next of kin was of the age of 40 years and more. Seyntcler's counsel had obtained a copy of this inquisition and were ready to have the original produced in court. Lydeyard therefore suborned an Exchequer clerk called Broket to go to the Tower of

London (where such records were then kept) and erase the figures xl (=40) and then to re-write the xl with fresh ink and a blot to make it look suspect. Suspicion fell on a lawyer called Robert Danvers who was counsel for Seyntcler, and he in turn now engaged in a little forgery himself: he sent Broket a letter purporting to come from Broket's employer, Lydeyard, and asking whether Broket might have been observed when he made the erasure, as rumours were suggesting. Broket obligingly sent back a thoroughly incriminating reply, thus shifting the entire weight of evidence to the other side.

Given the ingenuity of the forger, it is perhaps unsurprising that the law courts and royal officials were reluctant to be drawn into the critical examination of documents that came before them. The Chancery, it has been said, 'would confirm and exemplify almost anything',[29] although its officials did occasionally examine documents to see if they were forged (probably relying on finding whether copies of them were enrolled in the Chancery records).[30] Law courts were more often obliged to investigate claims of forgery, especially after the passing of the relevant statutes (which of course opened the floodgates to spurious claims of forgery), but it is notable that the courts took a remarkably lenient view of forgery where their own authority was being impugned. For instance, a forged warrant of arrest in 1497 cost the offender only a fine of *6s. 8d.* in the King's Bench.[31]

The danger of forgery was obviously enhanced in a society whose legal system placed great credence in the merits of 'specialty' (documents under seal) and yet where many members of the society were illiterate. A late 14th-century record will illustrate what I mean. It was stated by two ecclesiastics of Wyke near Pershore, in Worcestershire, that at about midnight one night Emma Calawe, the wife of John Hayward the elder, seeing her husband at death's door, had sent for Thomas Sampson, chaplain. Thomas had written a false charter of John's lands and tenements, whereby John gave them all to Emma forever, and Emma, Thomas and her son (whom she was disinheriting) then took a silver button from her hood and put it in John's hand, and took his hand and laid it on the false deed, John being insensible.[32]

How were illiterates to be able to trust in the honesty of people who wrote things for them? From the 13th century onwards, the Church evinced strong objections to clergy of the grade of subdeacon or above engaging in secular employment.[33] And yet, especially from about the mid 14th-century onwards, increasing reliance was put on written documents. There was a multiplication of legal documentation, especially in the Chancery, there was increasing use of bonds in commercial life, written leases became common as demesne cultivation of estates declined, and the making of written testaments and wills became commonplace. Equally, care was needed in the preparation of such documentation, as the legislation of Edward I's reign was assimilated by the law courts and interpreted and adapted.

One result of such trends was the rise of the professional scrivener. The professional writer of books had been around since the 12th century, and in the course of the 13th century those who wrote in Oxford and Cambridge had tended to come under the regulation and jurisdiction of the universities in those towns. But I would distinguish these booktrade members from the writers of documents: the work of the two categories of professional writers was different in substance as well as in form.[34] Besides, the evidence for the scriveners is concentrated in London, although of course they are early found in both Oxford and Cambridge, and in other towns too.

Forgery cases are, as it happens, some of the earlier indications of scriveners' activities in London. For instance, in 1365–6 Robert de Ednesore, scrivener, was found guilty in the Husting of Pleas of Land, London, of having in Fleet Street (perhaps where he lived) forged two deeds. He was condemned to the pillory, to stand there for two hours, with the deeds hung by a string from his neck; he was not set at liberty until he had sworn that he would never again consent or incline to such forgery.[35] The case is remarkable for showing the City's readiness to punish a forger of private deeds, thus making up for the statute and common law's deficiencies. Comparably, in 1376 William Grendone or Credelle, scrivener, was committed to Newgate for making false indentures of apprenticeship.[36]

Such cases must have highlighted the need for regulation of the London scriveners' craft. The scriveners themselves were painfully aware of this, for in 1373 they had drawn up rules for their craft, which were accepted for enrolment of the Guildhall.[37] The preamble of these rules refers to the problem of the

> 'mischiefs and defaults that are, and have often been committed in the said craft by those who resort to the City from divers countries, as well chaplains and others, who have no knowledge of the customs, franchises and usage of the said City, and who call themselves scriveners, and undertake to make wills, charters and all other things touching the said craft; the fact being that they are . . . less skilled than the scriveners who are free of the City and who for a long time have been versed in their craft.'

The principal remedies were stated as being: a monopoly of scriveners in the City for the members of the craft, the examination of all would-be members of the craft by other members of it, and the putting of his name to his deeds by every member of the craft.

These regulations were not a complete success. The 'signing' of names was later said to have been followed for no more than three years;[38] it is no doubt to be seen as a reflection of the practice of notaries of putting their elaborate mark on every instrument that they drew up. (It was only within the last generation that notaries had become at all well known in English diplomatic practice). The idea may also have owed something to the practice of goldsmiths, armourers, turners and members of other City crafts, of affixing their mark to their products.

I think that the late 14th century must be seen as the critical period for the emergence of the London scriveners as a well-regulated professional body: the process took about a generation.

In 1380 a testament (or will) was said to have been forged by one Doncastre, scrivener, at his premises in Lombard Street[39] – although it is not clear if he had any criminal intent – while in 1384 Adam Stedeman, scrivener, who was apparently employed by a London goldsmith to write his will, inserted a clause appointing himself executor.[40] Stedeman was obliged to acknowledge in full Husting that he had done this knowing that it was contrary to his employer's wish, and to renounce administration. But it was perhaps a further scandal, in 1391, that led to the second overhaul of the scriveners' craft. Thomas Pantier is said in the scriveners' own records to have been 'a foreigner, who had been a hireling with a scrivener for two years and was never apprenticed; he began to hold shop . . . and within a quarter of a year . . ., through lack of knowledge and ignorance of the science of the said craft, he was sent to the pillory'. The City's records indicate that he had written two false deeds, endorsing them as having been enrolled in the Hustings court several years previously, and being a party to the familiar trick of transferring two genuine wax seal impressions to the false deeds. He was sentenced to stand in the pillory for an hour, and was afterwards (presumably by the scriveners' craft) banned from following his calling of scrivener within the city.[41]

The scriveners' craft, now thus revived, never again ceased to maintain its organisation. New ordinances were drawn up a year after Pantier's case, with regulations that would reduce the risk of forgery.[42]

It is, however, worth remarking that the scriveners regarded it as entirely acceptable to draw up deeds that bore a different date from the true date of their execution.[43] The 1373 regulations had apparently met with opposition because of the common practice of dates being added subsequently to the drawing-up of deeds, and the 1392 ordinances simply forbad the making of a deed that was to be sealed bearing a date a *long* time before or after its making, or of closed letters of a date *far distant*.[44] This may have reflected the need for, say, deeds relating to livery of seisin to be dated when the transaction was completed, but it is difficult to avoid the feeling that the scriveners were laying themselves open to charges of bad intent.

From about 1392, too, the scriveners began to record the names of their members in a book, still surviving, known as their Common Paper. It is astonishing that it is not more consulted, and indeed that it has not been printed in facsimile, for it contains the signatures and whole sentences in the handwriting of all the craft's members from this date onwards, sometimes with a notarial mark or a scrivener's paraph added too.[45]

That the regulations were a success, or at least that the scriveners now became a respectable and trusted profession can be deduced from the fact that no member of the company is known to have been found guilty of forgery in the 15th century. Instead, what is evident is an expansion of the range of activities engaged in by the craft.

A good many 15th-century scriveners were also notaries public, by papal or imperial authority, or both, and although it is quite unclear how far notaries were examined for professional competence at this date,[46] it is (and was) perhaps a fair presumption that since their mere handwritten mark was as good as specialty for an ecclesiastical court or for any continental jurisdiction, they were likely to be entirely honest. The total number of scriveners admitted to the company increased from the 1460s onwards, and the range of activities that they undertook seems to have widened. They became more like legal draftsmen at times, preparing documentation for Chancery suits and holding minor legal offices; it was by no means rare, either, for them to be asked to act as executors of the wills that they drew up, or as feoffees. Richard Whittington (*d.*1423) can be seen as a trendsetter in this respect, for he made William Grove, scrivener of London, one of his executors, and Grove acted in this capacity for several years.[47] Grove is shown among those standing around Whittington at his deathbed, in a picture on the first page of the ordinances of Whittington's Charity.

It probably became the common practice for 15th-century scriveners to keep books of summaries or memoranda of the documents that they had drawn up, and these came to be regarded as valid evidence in mercantile custom;[48] in keeping such books, the 15th-century scriveners further resembled notaries, who had always been accustomed to keep memoranda of the instruments they drew up and authenticated. And finally it may be suggested that the high level of trust that people felt they could put in scriveners' honesty is demonstrated by their rise as brokers. If in the 15th century one wanted to have an obligation or other bond drawn up, one went to a scrivener's shop, and I have the impression that those in Lombard Street were the ones that specialized in the drawing up of such financial instruments.[49] It was only a stage or so further in the process for people to entrust the custody of completed bonds or, next, of actual sums of money to the scriveners. That was to be the London scriveners' supreme success.

References

1. The literature on forgery in medieval England is not abundant; see, however, C.N.L. Brooke, 'Approaches to Medieval Forgery', *Journal Soc. of Archivists*, iii (1965–9), pp.377–86, reprinted in his collected essays, *The Medieval Church and Society* (London, 1971), pp.100–20; L.C. Hector, *Palaeography and Forgery*, St Anthony's Hall Publications, No.15 (London and York, 1959); J. Röhrkasten, 'Zur Behandlung der Fälschung im englischen Strafrecht des Mittelalters', in *Fälschungen im Mittelalter. Internationaler Kongress der Monumenta Germaniae Historica, München, 16.–19. September*

1986 (= *Monumenta Germaniae Historica Schriften*, xxxiii, 1988), ii, *Gefälschte Rechtstexte – Der bestrafte Fälscher*, pp.627–59.

2. The rise of professional scribes is touched on at various angles by M.T. Clanchy, *From Memory to Written Record, England 1066–1307* (London, 1979) [hereafter Clanchy, *From Memory to Written Record*].
3. For notaries in England see C.R. Cheney, *Notaries Public in England in the Thirteenth and Fourteenth Centuries* (Oxford, 1972) [hereafter Cheney, *Notaries Public*], and id., 'Notaries Public in Italy and England in the Late Middle Ages', *Studi Senesi*, 3rd ser., xxix (= xcii) (1980), pp.173–88.
4. See Clanchy, *From Memory to Written Record*, index, *s.v. signum*.
5. It was also common to use someone else's seal (e.g. that of the local mayor) if one's own seal was not well enough known: for an instance from as late as 1503 see *Cal. Close* R., *Henry VII*, ii, *1500–9*, pp.178–9, no.455.
6. U. Berlière, 'Le Sceau Conventuel', *Revue Bénédictine*, xxxviii (1926), pp.228–309, discusses the controls operated within monastic houses. People who lost their seal-matrix sometimes sought to publicise the loss, to as to prevent credence in impressions made from the seal: e.g. *Calendar of Close* R*olls, 1318–23*, p.628 (bis), for proclamation of loss and then discovery of Privy Seal.
7. For the use of counterseals see H. Appelt, 'Über Kontrasigilla mittelalterlicher Urkundenschreiber', *Mitteilungen des Instituts für österreichische Geschichtsforschung*, lix (1951), pp.118–22; B. Bédos, 'L'emploi du contre-sceau au Moyen Age: l'exemple de la sigillographie urbaine', *Bibliothèque de l'École des Chartes*, cxxxviii (1981), pp.161–78.
8. *The treatise on the laws and customs of the realm of England commonly called Glanvill*, ed. G.D.G. Hall (London, etc., 1965) [hereafter *Glanvill*], pp.176–7 (lib. xiv, c.7).
9. See F.S. Lear, *Treason in Roman and Germanic Law* (Austin, Texas, 1965), p.119; for the general influence of the Roman *crimen laesae maiestatis* on medieval concepts of treason see S.H. Cuttler, *The Law of Treason and Treason Trials in Later Medieval France* (Cambridge, etc., 1981), chapter 1.
10. Stat. 25 Edward III, c.2; *Statutes of the Realm*, 11 volumes (Record Commission, 1810–28) [hereafter *S.R.*], i, pp.319–20.
11. See, for instance, J.G. Bellamy, *The Law of Treason in England in the Later Middle Ages* (Cambridge, 1970), pp.134, 235. The construction was nevertheless not always expected by either forgers or jurors: see, for instance, *Select Cases in the Court of King's Bench* . . . , ed. G.O. Sayles, vii (Selden Soc., lxxxviii, 1971), p.107.
12. F. Pollock and F.W. Maitland, *History of English Law before the Time of Edward I*, 2nd edn., reprinted with an introduction by S.F.C. Milsom (Cambridge, 1968), ii, p.504n.
13. *Dictionnaire de Droit Canonique*, ed. R. Naz et al., 7 vols. (Paris, 1935–65), v, cols. 816–22, s.v. Faux. The papacy also developed elaborate diplomatic means of ensuring authenticity for papal missives, to combat the widespread practice of forging papal letters.

14. This lack of protection had not always been the case, if one can accept the statement in *Glanvill*, p.177 (lib. xiv, c.7); cf. also the late 13th century treatise, *Britton*, ed. F.M. Nichols, 2 vols. (Oxford, 1865), i, pp.40–1.
15. *Curia Regis Rolls . . . 8–10 John* [1207–9] (London, 1931), p.22. Similarly *Glanvill*, p.127 (lib.x c.12).
16. Cf. *Bracton on the Laws and Customs of England*, transl. S.E. Thorne, 4 vols. (Cambridge, Mass., 1968–77) [hereafter *Bracton*], ii, p.109, and, more generally, Clanchy, *From Memory to Written Record*, chapters 5 and 9.
17. *Rotuli Parliamentorum; ut et Petitiones et Placita in Parliamento,* 6 vols. (n.p., n.d. [London, 1767–77]) [hereafter *Rot. Parl.*], ii, p.308, no.45.
18. See Stat. 5 Henry IV, c.14; *S.R.*, ii, p.147. For the forgery of fines themselves, see H. G. Richardson, 'The Forgery of Fines, 1272–1376', *English Historical Review*, xxxv (1920), pp.405–18.
19. *Calendar of Patent Rolls, 1348–50*, pp.74–5; *ibid., 1385–9*, p.389, and cf. p.257; cf. also *ibid., 1429–36*, p.607.
20. See, for instance, the Early Chancery Proceedings, Public Record Office, C.1/9/285, 9/357–61, 14/24 and 15/18; *Calendar of Proceedings in Chancery in the Reign of Elizabeth, with Earlier Examples*, 3 vols. (Record Commission, 1827–32), ii, pp.xxx, xxxi.
21. Stat. 1 Henry V, c.3; and cf. stat. 7 Henry V, c.2; *S.R.*, ii, pp.170–1, 202.
22. Stat. 27 Henry VIII, c.2; *S.R.*, iii, p.532.
23. J.G. Bellamy, *The Tudor Law of Treason* (London, etc., 1979), pp.60, 247 n.30
24. Stat. 5 Elizabeth I, c.14; *S.R.*, iv, pp.443–5.
25. For discussion of medieval awareness of different styles of script see Hector, *Palaeography and Forgery*, pp.13–14.
26. *Bracton*, iv, p.242; cf. *ibid.*, ii, p.109 (forged seal, or erasure, as indicating falsity).
27. Hector, *Palaeography and Forgery*, p.9.
28. J. F. Baldwin, *The King's Council in England during the Middle Ages* (Oxford, 1913), pp.525–9; printed with translation in *Select Cases before the King's Council, 1243–1482*, ed. I.S. Leadam and J.F. Baldwin (Selden Soc., xxxv, 1918), pp.97–101, and discussed in *ibid.*, pp.cviii–ix; Hector, *Palaeography and Forgery*, pp.16–18. Curiously enough, Hector was unaware of Baldwin's publication of the case.
29. V.H. Galbraith, *Historical Research in Medieval England* (London, 1951), p.41.
30. See e.g. *Cal. Pat. R., 1461–7*, p.527.
31. *Select Cases in the Council of Henry VIII*, ed. C.G. Bayne and W.H. Dunham (Selden Soc., lxxv, for 1956 (1958)), p.cliv, n.1. A forger of the seal of the court of Queen's Bench in 1571 was pilloried: Bellamy, *Tudor Law of Treason*, p.275, n.10.
32. *Descriptive Catalogue of Ancient Deeds in the Public Record Office*, v (London, 1906), pp.120–1.
33. See e.g. *Councils and Synods with other Documents relating to the English Church*, ii, *1205–1313*, ed. F.M. Powicke and C.R. Cheney, 2 parts (Oxford, 1964), pt.i, pp.26–7 (cc.9–10), 110 (c.12),and pt.ii, pp.754–5 (c.6).
34. In 13th- and 14th-century Oxford, deeds (and cartularies) and testaments seem

generally to have been written by clerks (including the town clerk) and scriveners, while the professional copying of books was the province of the *exemplarii* and stationers.

35. *Memorials of London and London Life in the XIIIth, XIVth and XVth Centuries . . .*, ed. H.T. Riley (London, 1868) [hereafter Riley, *Memorials*], pp.333–5.
36. *Calendar of Letter-Books . . . of the City of London . . . Letter-Book H*, ed. R.R. Sharpe (London, 1907), p.34; Riley, *Memorials*, p.397; for Grendon see also V.B. Redstone, 'The Chaucers of Suffolk', in *Memorials of Old Suffolk*, ed. V.B. Redstone (London, 1908), p.249 and plate opp. p.244.
37. *Scriveners' Company Common Paper, 1357–1628 . . .*, ed. F.W. Steer (London Record Society, iv, 1968) [hereafter *Common Paper*], p.2.
38. *Ibid.*, p.3.
39. Doncastre is to be identified with Robert Dancastre, who practised in London at this time. For the forgery, see *Select Cases before the King's Council, 1243–1482*, ed. I.S. Leadam and J.F. Baldwin (Selden Society, xxxv, 1918), p.73.
40. *Calendar of Wills proved and enrolled in the Court of Husting, London, A.D. 1258–A.D. 1688 . . .*, ed. R.R. Sharpe, 2 parts (London, 1889–90), ii, p.245.
41. Riley, *Memorials*, pp.527–9. Pantier may never have returned to being a scrivener; in 1425–6 the accounts of the Merchant Taylors Company include a gift of 4*s*. 8*d*. to him, *jadis* (formerly, or once) scrivener of London.
42. *Common Paper*, pp.4, 5–8.
43. *Ibid.*, pp.3, 62–3.
44. *Ibid.*, p.6.
45. The text of the Common Paper (London, Guildhall Library, MS 5370) was printed in F.W. Steer's edition, *Common Paper*; a few of the scriveners' paraphs and notarial marks were reproduced by E. Freshfield, 'Some Notarial Marks in the "Common Paper" of the Scriveners' Company', *Archaeologia*, liv (1895), pp.239–54, and by H. Jenkinson, *The Later Court Hands in England* (Cambridge, 1927).
46. Cheney, *Notaries Public*, chapter 6.
47. J. Imray, *The Charity of Richard Whittington* (London, 1968), pp. 6, 13, 30.
48. M.M. Postan gathered together some evidence from Chancery equitable proceedings and argued that scriveners' books were seen as 'valid evidence in merchant custom, and possibly in the courts of the Chancery and the Exchequer' in his 'Private Financial Instruments in Medieval England', *Vierteljahrschrift für Sozial- und Wirtschaftsgeschichte*, xxiii (1930), pp.26–75, reprinted in his *Medieval Trade and Finance* (Cambridge, 1973), pp.28–64, at 34–5.
49. There are several references to notaries (who were also scriveners) acting in Lombard Street, from 1459 onwards, in the *Calendars of State Papers, Venetian*, i and iii: Peter Bonamitie, Robert Cressy, John Devereux, Thomas Kyffyn and William Slade.

I am grateful to Dr Caroline Barron and Dr Martha Carlin for their suggestions and comments.

The Forgery of Printed Documents

Nicolas Barker

I BEGIN WITH an observation, not on printed documents alone as such, but in the general context of the forensic examination of documents, in their widest sense; that is to say, including any kind of human artefact. I was reading in one of the papers the other day the assertion by a curator of such documents that an important aspect of their analysis was what he called 'curator's eye'. Now this, of course, sounds instantly suspect. It is our old friend subjective judgement: 'I have seen more paintings by Rembrandt than anyone else in the world and I know'. But, on the other hand, take what is too slackly called forensic evidence. Forensic evidence means only evidence that will stand up in a court of law. Now the point to which I wish to draw attention is not the superior accuracy of such evidence, but its extraordinary limitations. There is a very great deal more evidence which is not forensic, but is nonetheless evidence and I see this *contrapposto* between 'I see with my little eye, and my eye is better than yours', and, on the other hand, 'it fluoresces, therefore it must be wrong' as a kind of balance of evidence, a pendulum effect. At any period, faced with any particular concatenation of circumstances that leads you to ask 'Is this right or wrong?', the pendulum will swing more in one direction than the other, but you should not despise one class of evidence because it is 'subjective' any more than you should adhere strongly to another body of evidence because it is 'objective'.

In fact, the truth about the validity of any object, as indeed of any statement, is that it is a summary of all the facts about it, observable or discoverable: about its structure, about the materials of which it is comprised, the methods used to make it or subsequently to alter it, and, beyond those physical facts, beliefs, because obviously beliefs as to the genuineness or otherwise of an object are an important factor in their history. And this brings us to the question of motive. Again, one has to disentangle the forensic view of a motive, which is that fraud was or was not intended. Real life is often more complicated than this. An object which started off as perfectly genuine, a pious imitation perhaps of another object, becomes, with the passage of time, the subject of deliberate fraud, so that when one is talking about forgery or non-forgery one has a complicating time continuum to consider.

This last factor is a particularly difficult problem when one is confronted with printed documents. There is a phenomenon, very well known to most of you: if a second compositor is required to set up again what a previous compositor has set up, it is vastly easier and simpler for him to ape the size of the letter, the length of the line, the number of lines per page, in the earlier setting. Why? Because it is so much quicker: you can get through the work far more rapidly than if you have to re-cast it off and make all the decisions about justification over again. It is a truism to anybody who deals in printed documents in the 16th and 17th and 18th centuries (and I daresay the 15th century), that there are in existence many more reprints from standing type, which are in fact complete re-settings, than we have any idea of at all. So with that initial obfuscating cloud of complexity to lay before you, we will plunge straight away into my own very modest experience of this sort of thing.

I first got involved in the consideration of typographic forgery in 1972; in fact, to be absolutely exact, I think it was the 8th of May 1972 because it was on the 1st of May 1972 that Messrs Sotheby's put up for sale a collection of pamphlets printed by Frederic Prokosch, which were described as 'the property of a gentleman' (a characteristic piece of anonymity which was perhaps itself a forgery on this occasion), and were described as the only complete set of all the pamphlets produced by Frederic Prokosch, among them no less than 50 separate printed titles. Frederic Prokosch, I later discovered, was a very interesting man: he had been admitted very early on to a kind of charmed circle of international distinction in literature; he introduced himself to Masefield, and De La Mare, in the late 1920s, and had become the intimate friend of Auden and Spender, both more or less his own age; he had not been slow to make the acquaintance of T.S. Eliot, Thomas Mann, and others, and he had formed the agreeable habit of taking a poem recently sent to him by one of his friends and having a few, a very few, copies of it printed as a kind of glorified Christmas card. He would send all (or nearly all) these copies with the request that their author would autograph one copy for himself and please distribute the rest to his friends. Few authors are immune to flattery, and I think that, without exception, all the authors to whom he addressed these things took them in good part. I suppose you could say that they were an act of literary piracy, but that would be perhaps taking an unnecessarily severe view of things.

I think no one in the sale room had any idea that so many as 50 of these pamphlets might have been printed, but then they didn't, in the nature of their rarity, come up for sale very often and when they did, because they were about the size of a book of postage stamps, they tended to be kept in envelopes into which people didn't look very often. So it happened that, if not very many people had seen them (although they might have handled them), still fewer people had looked at them very hard. As luck would have it, the vast majority were bought by Bernard Quaritch, who almost immediately bundled up those by T.S. Eliot and took them over to Harvard where there is the world's best collection of T.S. Eliot, including copies of everything that he wrote given by the poet, a punctilious archivist of his own work. It was rather disconcerting, therefore, to find that a number of these little books by Eliot were not at Harvard. Arthur Freeman, for it was he who had undertaken this mission, committed the first and crucial step in the process that followed by actually taking the booklets out of their envelopes and arranging them in order. As he did so he noticed that some of them lay flat, while others seemed oddly springy. They would open up as he laid them on the table. So I hasten to point out that Arthur made the first crucial jump from acceptance and suspicion; I didn't do it – he did.

But, when he came home with suspicion in his mind, he sent for me and very quickly these were the images that were presented to me among others. On the one hand we had a book printed in 1935, set in the then still fairly new Perpetua type by the Cambridge University Press (Prokosch had a research scholarship at King's College, Cambridge, at the time) and on the other hand we had an object allegedly printed in Lisbon (he spent the last months in Europe, from which he was very reluctant to retreat during the War, at Estoril in Portugal), but in a type which I had no hesitation in identifying as one called Aster which had been produced by the Italian type foundry of Simoncini, in, I felt sure, more recent times. A quick glance at the *Encyclopedia of Type Faces* revealed that it was in fact in 1958. You don't need to go too far into the intricacies of the Roman numeral system to work out that this posed something of a problem.

What happened next owes vastly more to Nigel Seeley, who was then at the Scotland Yard Forensic Department and is now the lecturer at the Institute of Archaeology, than to me. Having very early on established that there were a lot of wrong 'uns in this lot, we then went to town on the testing techniques, for which we had the example of Carter and Pollard to guide us. First of all we tested the paper. We found that before the War, at the alleged date, what are now known as optical dyes, that is the blueish fluorescent dye that makes your whites bluer than Mrs X's, did not exist; we also found that, although the thread used was entirely pure cotton thread, you could see, under an electron microscope magnification, here and there the tiniest thread of man-made fibre spun in. Now it is virtually impossible to run a spinning mill in which pure cotton and pure man-made fibres are spun. You may advertise what you are selling as 100% pure cotton, but what is floating in the air, rather than lying on the floor, will tend to get absorbed in the spinning process.

The marbling turned out to be interesting too. Pre-war papers were mostly marbled by hand, and one of the main suppliers of marbled paper on the continent, the firm of Keller, Dorian, Putois, had supplied some of the marbled papers used before the War and the same design after the War. However, their plant had been completely destroyed during the War, and instead of having the traditional hand-marbling baths, they had introduced a thermographic marbling machine. Thermographic marbling and hand marbling are actually quite easy to tell apart, even if the effect is essentially, to the lay eye, the same.

The gold foil, on the other hand, was one of our failures. There were little labels on the front board of these pamphlets, many printed on a very bright shiny gold foil. I thought I recognised a very modern phenomenon here, the result of the application of vacuum extraction. Vacuum extracted foil was a product of wartime needs; some of you may remember those ribbons of silver foil dropped to deflect radar, which were produced by the vacuum extraction process which was developed in 1940–41. It turned out that I was entirely wrong, because the foils used were old-fashioned rolled gold and silver paper. What was so new about them was that they had been coated with nitro-cellulose varnish, which is very shiny and gives the effect of tremendously high-gloss metal. Nitro-cellulose varnishing has been in existence since the late 1860s. The fact that nitro-cellulose varnish was only used, as far as I can make out, in the making of high gloss foil paper from about 1960 onwards cannot be proved. Finally, each pamphlet was enclosed in transparent plastic covers which turned out to be made of polyvinyl chloride – a substance not in existence before the War.

There are two immediate lessons to be drawn from this little tale, both with rather larger implications. The first is that time is of the essence: that is to say, establishing that an object is or is not a forgery must be related to time. This is very important with printed books and the implications will become clearer, but if you produce one piece of printed matter in 1900 and another piece 30 years later, bearing exactly the same words, set in the same type, printed on the same paper and also dated 1900, you have committed piracy, but have you committed forgery? Then there is the sub-issue of the wording of the imprint on the title page. If it says by Messrs G Redwood and you are not Messrs G Redwood, then presumably again you have committed forgery. If this were all, forgery would be easy to define and easy to do. But this is where the time factor comes in. Within this time continuum, huge human upheavals – war, vast expansions in economic demand for some commodity – will lead to changes which leave their mark on the way people make things. These marks are not charted and will not be recognized by a potential forger, unless he is very clever indeed (I shall be coming in a moment to an example of a forger who is very clever indeed). Finally, I must repeat in the context of this time continuum that you can be as clever as you like and still not spot the most innocent of imitations.

Keith Fletcher has got a forgery (although it is not a forgery, but an honest copy, signed in a microscopic hand) of one of the famous early tracts on the discovery of America. Anybody in this audience would look at that book and swear that it was a piece of 16th-century printing, and yet, when you look at the end, it says in tiny letters 'J. Harris facsim:'. Now the interesting thing, and probably the most effective form of deceit to our eye, lies in the fact that most people in the 19th century washed early printed books when they came into their hands. So when we look at this book in its Bedford binding, it gives the impression of a piece of 16th-century printing which has had all the guts, the 16th-century-ness, of it washed out, and we don't see that it is merely Harris's idea of what a piece of 16th-century printing looked like in his time. So the special factor of time makes a special demand for alertness in the person who is going to spot a typographic forgery.

Without more ado I will pass on, and come to two old acquaintances of mine, and yours, too, I daresay. There you have them; the very image of hypocrisy, Harry Buxton Forman, and Thomas James Wise, every inch a commercially successful bounder. I hardly need rehearse here the classic qualities of *An Enquiry into the Nature of Certain Nineteenth-century Pamphlets*, and only remind you of the very important distinction drawn there between negative and positive evidence of forgery. Negative evidence depends on the fact that no known copy is known with the author's signature or in a contemporary binding, that there is no mention in the correspondence of the author of the time, or anywhere else. All the negative evidence was compelling, although not in itself sufficient. The positive evidence is based on the facts that prove a pamphlet could not have existed at the material time. For example, it may be printed on paper which could not have existed at the time. Paper was made from rags until esparto grass was introduced in 1861; wood pulp paper is a slightly more complicated issue, but it was not commercially available before 1880. These facts served to condemn over 30 of these pamphlets, because they were printed on paper which could not possibly have existed at the date on the title page.

Then there was the text. The classic case of this was Ruskin's 'The Queen's Gardens'. Ruskin went up to Manchester just about Christmas in 1864, and gave a speech which was reported *in extenso* in the *Manchester Examiner and Times*. This appeared again in *Sesame and Lilies* in 1866. *Sesame and Lilies* was reprinted in 1867 and 1868, and Ruskin revised it for the first time substantially for his *Collected Works* in 1871. Lo and behold, much later on appeared that black swan, a specially privately printed pamphlet text of 'The Queen's Gardens' run off in a few copies only by a local Manchester printer in 1864, and what is the text? It is the text as revised by Ruskin in 1871, not the text as given by Ruskin in 1864 whose authenticity we can trace from the *Manchester Examiner* of that very day through the successive editions of *Sesame and Lilies*. So the text is positive evidence of forgery.

And, finally, there is type, and the famous 'Clay's Long Primer No. 3'. It first appears in the April 1877 number of *Macmillan's Magazine*. Long Primer No. 3 was a curious type because it wasn't a book-work type at all; it was a newspaper type. Richard Clay III was a very interesting and innovative character who had been one of the first people to put in typesetting machinery; he had discovered that kerns, the projecting tails of 'f' and 'j', were frequently damaged by typesetting machinery. He saw in Stevens and Shanks's list of newspaper types that they had already developed one with a special 'f' and 'j' with the curve bent back so that it did not kern. And we can tell pretty exactly when Clay's in fact introduced it, from that issue of *Macmillan's Magazine* for April 1877. If one looks at what was clearly standing type held over from the previous issue, in the predecessor of Long Primer No. 3, Millar and Richard's Long Primer No. 28; it has its own proper and identifiable question mark, which is like a meat hook. Looking at the new copy set in May, one has the first appearance of Clay's Long Primer No. 3 with the button hook 'f' and 'j', but without Stevens and Shanks's question mark, which was of the non-meat hook variety, the one that looks like a saucepan with the dot on the end. If you ask why Clay's didn't bother to change the question mark, the answer is 'why should they?'. Both types were cast on a Long Primer body, and it saved on the typefounders' bill not to order another matrix for the question mark.

Next we have another example of typographic anachronism. Clay's Long Primer No.3 was the type that condemned *Sonnets from the Portuguese* and 15 other books which purported to have been printed before 1877. There is a pamphlet by Thackeray, *An Interesting Event*, which bears the date 1849 on the title page. The typographic evidence against this has been complicated by some misunderstanding abut the date of introduction of that most pervasive of late Victorian types, Miller and Richard's Old Style, in which it is set. Miller and Richard's Old Style was first cut by the great punchcutter Alexander Phemister, and the first publicity leaflet for it in the St Bride Printing Library, which has the biggest set of consecutive 19th-century type founders' specimens in the world, is dated 1860. This is interesting because F.W. Farrer's *Lyrics of Life* is set in Miller and Richard's Old Style, but dated 1859. I can only assume that, since Richard Clay did a substantial business with Miller and Richard, they had founts of it a year before they promoted it to the trade. Anyway, 1849 is too early.

The next example, Swinburne's *Siena*, is less arcane. This is what Graham Pollard christened a binary forgery, that is to say, a forgery of a known and genuine original, as opposed to the creative forgeries like *An Interesting Event* whose falsity was obscured by the fact that there was no known original. It may be a little hard to believe that every line of type and every ornament in the genuine and the forged *Siena* is set in a different kind of type, but it is easy to see that the word 'Siena' at the top is in two different sizes, and, most striking, that the genuine *Siena* has a drop initial which goes correctly from the top of cap height in the first line to the foot of the x-height in the second line, whereas the false has the drop initial lining at the top but not at the foot. You can also possibly just tell that the little ornament is not the same.

Another case has a special interest, because here you have what I believe to be the *fons et origo* of Wise and Forman's forgery. This is a perfectly genuine pamphlet, *Two Poems*, produced by Elizabeth and Robert Browning for Elizabeth's sister Arabel (who was much addicted to good causes), to be sold at a charity bazaar in 1854. Those of you who frequent charity bazaars will not be greatly surprised that it clearly didn't go very well, and Forman, who had a habit of digging in publishers' back cupboards, must have discovered a parcel containing some 300 unsold copies of this pamphlet. These he did not sell, at least originally, but used for swaps. So, when Wise called on him in January 1886 to examine his Shelley collection, Forman must have shown him the parcel, and, I suspect, introduced him to the concept of swaps. It was not very long thereafter that the first of what we may call the 'commercial' forgeries appeared.

It is very interesting that in 1916, at the end of their career, the last known contact between Wise and Forman shows that this idea was still current in their minds. Wise had just published his *Bibliography of Wordsworth*, in which he wrote that 'a little remainder' of *To the Queen* had been discovered and distributed among a few friends; and in writing to send a copy of his book to Forman he was at pains to explain that 'that little "remainder" that we divided' had now been destroyed. This suggests to me that 'remainder' was in fact a piece of slang between the two, a euphemism for 'forgery'.

This brings me back to *Two Poems*: had anybody said, 'Good heavens, Mr Wise and Mr Forman, where do these remarkably fresh copies, which seem to be appearing in such abundance, come from?', the answer would have been, 'Oh, a little remainder turned up in the publishers' back shop the other day'. At all events, there is a close resemblance between *Two Poems* 1854 and *The Runaway Slave at Pilgrim's Point* '1849', quite close enough to have laid any contemporary suspicion to rest. The only trouble is that the little semi-romanesque ornament in *The Runaway Slave* was issued along with Miller and Richard's Old Style and, like the type, promoted as brand new for the first time in 1860. As you will see, the date on the pamphlet is 1849.

The forgers were not always so careful, especially at the end of their career. The typographic appearance of Wordsworth's impassioned diatribe against the bringing of railways to the lakes, as genuinely printed by R. Branthwaite and Sons in 1846, must have been known to them. But no attempt has been made in *To the Queen*, apparently also printed by Branthwaite, to match it. Instead, it is in the sort of pamphlet style that Clays would have used had you sent them, as Wise no doubt did, a text not in book form and asked them to make a pamphlet of it. It has 1890 to 1900 written all over it: it is a bad forgery.

Not all the forgeries were printed by Clay. *The Books of William Morris,* one of Forman's curious essays in bibliography, for which he developed the interesting and unusual tactic of reproducing title pages in virtual type-facsimile, led to the source of another group of forgeries, all from the same source. *The Manifesto of the Socialist League* 1885 exists in two forms, one genuine, the other false. There are a number of interesting features about this, purely from a typographical point; the two wavy rules are quite different, as are the two black-letter types for 'Socialist League Office'. It is also noticeable that the types used for the forgery are exactly the same as the types used in the description of the pamphlet in Forman's book; there again the types used for forgery revealed the printer, Messrs Billing of Guildford, who printed *The Books of William Morris*. Notice also that the title block, an original wood block cut from a design by Walter Crane, has some rough marks left in to give an antique appearance. The forgery has the block reproduced by photo-engraving, and the block maker, seeing these unsightly marks, decided that he could do a good deal better than that and removed most of them, a piece of craftsman-like tidiness that further betrays the forgery.

Next comes what we may call an extension of the Clay's Long Primer No. 3 theory. The importance of Clay's Long Primer No. 3 was that it was a type peculiar to Richard Clay: nobody has found any other printer with that particular *combination* of types in use at that time. *The God of the Poor* '1884' presents a rather similar problem. It purports to be printed in 1884, but there is another pamphlet, *How I became a Socialist* by William Morris with an obituary notice of him, which was printed after his death in 1896 by a firm called the Twentieth Century Press, and is set in the same type. The Twentieth Century Press was actually founded to print the first edition of the Socialist *Manifesto* in 1893. I could not at first identify the type in which the two little books were set; eventually, after a great deal of rummaging, I discovered that it was a long primer cut by Vincent Figgins, but neither their Long Primer No. 11 nor yet the Long Primer no. 15, but a *mélange* of both. In fact, it contains 15 characters from Long Primer No. 11, 14 characters from Long Primer No. 15, and 15 which are common to both. I do not believe that a similar mixture of the two types exists elsewhere, and it follows that it can only have been made up for the Twentieth Century Press when it was started in 1893. Therefore it cannot have been available in 1884 when *The God of the Poor* was alleged to have been printed.

Finally, let us turn to an example of Forman's typographic skills at its best. He was an inveterate camp follower of distinguished writers, and in that capacity became Richard Hengist Horne's literary executor. To help and please Horne, he produced a number of pieces of his, among them *Galatea Secunda* '1867'. Some copies of this have the imprint 'Printed for private circulation', while others have 'Melbourne: G. Robertson, H.T. Dwight, S. Mullen'. Both are dated 1867: some of the copies are, rather curiously, printed on paper water-marked 1873. There is the same problem about books on paper which actually bear a date later than the title page as of books on paper whose constituents didn't exist at the time.

There are two other interesting things about *Galatea Secunda*. In the first place, it matches *The South Sea Sisters* as closely and carefully as *The Runaway Slave at Pilgrim's Point* matches *Two Poems*, thus strengthening the argument for Forman's hand in both. What is also interesting is that this is the first forgery to appear in commerce. It was sold with five other pamphlets in a lot at a sale of Forman's books in November 1884 after Horne had died and left him all his books. Forman was obviously rationalizing his collection and this booklet, with five others in a bundle, fetched only 2 shillings. No one can describe that as profiteering, and it is for that reason that I have a somewhat ambivalent view of Forman's guilt in a commercial sense whereas I have none about Wise's. I am left with the conviction that Wise's contribution to the partnership was not editorial ability of which he had very little, or aesthetic taste of which he had, if anything, rather less, but a commercial sense of the possibilities for making money which Forman completely lacked.

That brings us forward a century to our own time, to a crime as grave or graver than Wise and Forman's, which we may be thankful had a shorter run before it was identified. *The Oath of a Freeman* was the centrepiece of the activity of Mark Hofmann of Salt Lake City. Hofmann is now in his mid thirties. He was born in Salt Lake City, the son of an extremely devout Mormon who was secretary of his local branch of the church and in that capacity notable for the beauty, accuracy and neatness with which he used to keep the handwritten records of the church's business. His son, like most Mormons, did his standard two years as a missionary, in Bristol in England. The Mormon missionaries' work has a regular feature, the tracing of ancestors for retrospective baptism. It involves looking up old church registers, going to record offices and anywhere else where you can find large lists of names of people who existed in time past. Hofman says (but one has to treat everything he says with enormous caution because he is a pathological liar) that he first got his taste for what he did from studying old documents for this purpose. He came back to Salt Lake City and, by his own account (but again, one must be sceptical), from reading Fawn Brodie's *No Man Knows My History*, a rather critical biography of Joseph Smith, at some point he not only lost his faith but developed a violent distaste for it.

Now, at any rate, he set to work to forge documents – manuscript documents at first – which fell into two classes: those that triumphantly proved hitherto undocumented but essential tenets of the Mormon faith, and others which, more embarrassingly, failed to substantiate or contradicted the same type of tenet. You might think that this might have been a counterproductive policy, and I can only explain its efficacy by a rather crude analogy which appeared in an excellent summary of the Hofmann affair in the *Los Angeles Times*. Documents, ran the argument, mean a lot to the Mormons because their divine revelation is of such very recent date: it is as if the resurrection of Jesus Christ could be disproved by the existence of motel receipts showing he was elsewhere on Easter Saturday night. This explains the attitude of the Church. They behaved in a completely Pavlovian way. They had to buy the *pro* documents and trumpet them to the world; they had to buy the *anti* documents to suppress them, and they did.

Through these highly lucrative excursions into the gullibility of the Mormon Church, Hofmann was able to test out the gullibility of others. He got into the local trade in books, currency, and what are all too apt to be called 'memorabilia'. In the Rocky Mountains and Western America generally this trade revolves round local history, and the goods being in relatively short supply, they fetch very high prices, particularly bank notes. Very primitive wood-engraved and typeset banknotes were issued in the early days of what is now the state of Utah. Notes with a face value of 1 dollar, 2 dollars and 5 dollars for the Deseret Currency Association and the Western Boundary Bank were known to exist. Hofmann very quickly produced 10 dollar, 20 dollar and even 50 dollar denominations which nobody had ever seen before, and the dealers in currency swallowed them with avidity. From this, he moved into the book business; faking association copies of Mormon or Western interest became a growing part of his business which brought him increasingly into the national or East Coast rare book business.

Now the *Freeman's Oath*, perhaps the first piece of printed matter produced in North America, is known to have existed along with an almanac, both of which had already been printed, as the then Governor of Massachusetts noted their existence in his diary, by January 1639; but neither of them is known to survive. The first piece of printed matter in North America that does survive is the *Bay Psalm Book*, of which there are 8 copies, the last of which was sold for $151,000 in 1951.

So when Hofmann decided to produce the *Freeman's Oath* he had gone a long way up market. He set about it with characteristic ingenuity and thoroughness in March 1985. First, he had to create a provenance, and he 'planted' it on the Argosy Book Store in New York City. The Argosy Book Store has a large stock of 19th-century ephemera of every conceivable kind: ballads, election notices and so on. Hofmann was not so injudicious as to put the Oath itself among this; indeed, it was not in existence then. What he did was to take a copy of a patriotic ballad written in honour of Abraham Lincoln's re-election in 1863 and make a photograph of it; he removed its heading ('Give thanks, all ye people'), substituted for it a new heading reading 'The Oath of a Freeman', set in slightly irregular Clarendon caps, rephotographed it, printed it on a blank sheet of paper of *c.*1860, put it in a box in the Argosy Book Store, found it and had it sold to himself as 'The Oath of a Freeman', the title that was listed in the Argosy invoice. He thus had a genuine invoice which the Argosy Book Store was prepared to swear was issued by them.

He then set to work to create the *Oath* itself. He produced the original by photographing the pages of the *Bay Psalm Book* using the excellent 1956 Meriden facsimile. He enlarged these photographs and cut them up, letter by letter, sometimes using groups of conveniently adjacent letters, but very rarely whole words, creating the entire text of *The Oath of a Freeman*. He then reduced it down to the right size again and made a process line block. He knew that you can tell process block facsimiles from genuine type impressions because the height of the type is different, so he took a small industrial drill and ground down the height of letters individually on the block so that it would produce a slightly irregular impression. He made his own ink out of bee's-wax, carbon and linseed oil, making his carbon by burning 17th-century paper because he was afraid that carbon dating might catch him out. Finally, he printed it by laying a sheet of genuine 17th-century paper, a blank endleaf from a contemporary English book, on the surface of the inked block, and pressed it down, using an ordinary clamp and a padded board, moving the clamp along to produce a convincingly irregular impression.

So far it would be hardly possible to fault his technique. He actually created the thing in March 1985, and offered it to the Library of Congress in May, with the Schiller-Wapner Gallery acting as intermediary. A longish gap ensued while the Library of Congress examined it under magnification, ultra-violet and infra-red

THE OATH OF A FREEMAN.

I ·AB· being (by Gods providence) an Inhabitant,
and Freeman, within the iuriſdictiō of this
Common-wealth, doe freely acknowledge my
ſelfe to bee ſubject to the governement thereof;
and therefore doe heere ſweare, by the great
& dreadfull name of the Everliving-God, that
I will be true & faithfull to the ſame, & will
accordingly yield aſſiſtance & ſupport therunto,
with my perſon & eſtate, as in equity I am bo-
und: and will alſo truely indeavour to maintaine
and preſerve all the libertyes & privilidges there-
of, ſubmitting my ſelfe to the wholeſome lawes,
& ordres made & ſtabliſhed by the ſame; and fu-
rther, that I will not plot, nor practice any evill
againſt it, nor conſent to any that ſhall ſoe do,
butt will timely diſcover, & reveall the ſame to
lawefull authoritee nowe here ſtabliſhed, for the
ſpeedie preventing thereof. Moreover, I doe
ſolemnly binde my ſelfe, in the ſight of God,
that when I ſhalbe called, to give my voyce
touching any ſuch matter of this ſtate, (in wh-
ich freemen are to deale) I will give my vote
& ſuffrage as I ſhall judge in myne owne con-
ſcience may beſt conduce & tend to the publick
weale of the body, without reſpect of perſonn-
es, or favour of any man. Soe help mee God in
the Lord Ieſus Chriſt.

'The Oath of a Freeman', from a contact negative.

light, with raked illumination, testing it in every conceivable way. Ultimately, after two months or more, it returned the document to Hofmann, without establishing whether it was genuine or not, but simply saying that they were not satisfied as to title, in which they were absolutely right for not quite the reasons that they thought.

Hofmann, however, like many another over-confident fraudster, had spent the proceeds in advance and then embarked on a series of borrowings to finance his debt. Characteristically, he invented an archive which he alleged lay within his power to purchase. He raised more money on the strength of this and a whole card-castle of fraud developed which, as such things will, began to collapse. In October he betook himself to murder in a particularly unpleasant way. He murdered his principal and closest debtor with a drainpipe bomb and planted a similar drainpipe bomb on this man's partner whom he had never met, simply to create the illusion that both were victims of a disaffected creditor of the bank in which they both worked. In fact, he failed to murder the partner but killed the partner's wife instead. He was then about to plant a third bomb when it went off as he was about to handle it, or was in the process of handling it. Again, we will never get the truth of what was going on. Hofmann says it was his intention to blow himself up to deflect suspicion from himself. This must be nonsense because, since his plan was to suggest that the causes of this violent crime were something to do with the financial affairs of a bank with which he had nothing to do, blowing himself up would seem to be drawing attention to himself rather than the reverse.

Once again, it was chance and an unexpected concatenation of events that brought the forger to book. There he was, in hospital, blown up and unconscious, with detectives waiting at his bedside, all solicitude and anxiety. 'What happened?' they asked. 'I opened the door of my car', he said, 'something fell on the floor, and that's all I know'. This simple but mendacious statement instantly converted him from third victim to first suspect because the police could tell by the shape of the injuries on his legs that in fact he had been sitting in the car with the device on the seat beside him when it went off. So, rather as with Prokosch, the real case came to an end within seconds. There then followed the long and cumbrous business of making a case that would stand up in court. This was much complicated for the police by the defence lawyers. Hofmann was an inveterate liar, and his lawyers used his own tergiversations to confuse the true pattern of events. However, after protracted plea-bargaining, Hofmann was found guilty of murder and fraud, and sentenced to various terms of imprisonment from 5 years to life.

It was not until after this, in January 1987, that I was asked to look into the matter. I developed a number of arguments which proved, without reference to Hofmann's statements, that the *Oath* was a forgery. The first thing that strikes anybody familiar with 17th-century printing is that the alignment of the lines is very bad even by the standards of the worst typography of the period. What is not so immediately visible is the fact that the mis-alignment is not consistent with itself.

If you look at an example of distorted lines in the *Bay Psalm Book*, you will see that they make an even bowed shape, starting from the foot of the page and working up about 8 to 10 lines. The lines are all bowed the same way. Obviously, the furniture with which the form was locked up was green and warped under pressure, thus creating the bowed shape. Here, however, the misalignment is all over the place; there are a number of places where the letters actually overlap between lines. Metal types can be made to do strange things, but not, in the 17th century at least, to overlap each other.

Then there is the rather interesting business of the border. The *Bay Psalm Book* is divided into five books, and a set of border strips appears as the head piece of each of these five divisions. You can see that the compositor has arranged the first of these little arabesque ornaments in pairs and in the first case has treated them very simply, just a straightforward back-to-back line. In book two he has got a little more adventurous and inverted every second pair, giving a rather more varied pattern. He has repeated the same in the third book, though inverting the pattern of book two. He embarks apparently on the same pattern for book four, and inevitably the case has become somewhat confused by now and in two places he put not a pair but the same ornament repeated twice. When the printer reaches book five, he decided to revert to the easier pattern of book one which he achieves with the odd duplication at the end.

Hofmann's eye told him that there was something abnormal and different about book four; having an uncertain grasp of the realities of 17th-century printing, he instantly seized on this as an authenticating factor. People would be the more likely to believe that the *Oath* was the work of the same printers as the *Bay Psalm Book* if it had the same odd border. So he converted what was clearly an error in the *Bay Psalm Book* into what could only be a deliberate act in the border of the *Oath of a Freeman*. So that is another error of judgement.

The same problems affected the typographic arrangement as befell *Siena*. There are two-line initials for each psalm in the *Bay Psalm Book*. They were obviously meant to align with the top of the x-height at one line and the bottom of the x-height of the line below. The compositor, being ignorant as well as clumsy, did not grasp this, and set the first word in caps and the misalignment of the drop-initials follows automatically. Now you will see you also get a misalignment in *the Oath of a Freeman* but the 'I' is in an impossible position, aligning at the top of the cap height not at the x-height. Even if you turned the character upside down, that wouldn't work out. So that is another error.

There are further details. It is an odd fact there is only one 'ssi' ligature in the *Bay Psalm Book*, towards the end (Dd2). Normally, the 'ssi' ligatures were all made up by either having 's' followed by an 'si' ligature or an 'ss' ligature followed by an 'i'. Hofmann, however, created a false 'ssi', using two 's's of the same height: in the real thing, the first 's' is shorter than the second.

The parentheses are another example: like many a 17th-century printer,

Stephen Day only had one parenth which he used one way up at the beginning, and inverted at the end, so there is always a slight lack of alignment; here you have the parentheses both aligning. Finally, there is the very interesting case of the suspension marks. You can see the suspension marks, the missing ms and ns, as used in the *Bay Psalm Book*, only when there is a desperate need to save space and justification. Here the shape of the o is very conspicuous; it is too big. This big o is very markedly out of line with the rest of the fount, whereas the suspended o is appreciably smaller. In the fake *Oath* the o with its suspension mark is an ordinary o with a suspension mark drawn in. You will also notice that the justification is spectacularly wide here; there was absolutely no need to suspend the n. Again, it is a piece of *kitsch* authentication.

The last and really most decisive point is the text. There are three manuscript texts of the *Freeman's Oath* dating from 1634 to 1635. In none of them is 'Everliving-God' hyphenated, which poses the question why Hofmann's text is hyphenated. The answer lies with the translators. They must have had strong reasons, not yet explained, for rejecting the old Sternhold and Hopkins version, which would have been familiar and acceptable even to the early Massachusetts settlers. Some of their views are made clear in the preface, and one is that they were determined to represent the Hebrew text literally: where one word was used in Hebrew they wanted to have one word in English. There are some words in Hebrew which cannot be literally translated by one word in English, words with a reduplicative or strengthening sense, and verbs which require an added preposition in English. Thus, when they had a strengthened word, like 'strong God' instead of just 'God', they hyphenated it to indicate that it was one word in Hebrew; obviously, 'lift-up' and 'Glorious-King' are examples of this desire to indicate that there was one word only in the Hebrew. This is obviously a need or practice peculiar to the *Bay Psalm Book*, but it was seized on by Hofmann as another peculiarity which he could with advantage adapt to his needs, so he hyphenated 'Everliving-God' on the analogy of 'strong-God' and 'Glorious-King', without understanding the textual absurdity.

I have said that he very rarely used complete words, but he did on one or two occasions. The word 'libertyes' in line 12 of the *Oath* can be proved to have been taken entire (except for the last two letters) from the *Bay Psalm Book* (Cc 2, line 29). There is a unique thickening of ink in the counter of 'y', and the relative alignment of the characters is identical. The same word in the *Bay Psalm Book* close by (Cc 1v, line 20) is quite different.

Let me end with two facts about all this which put this impressive demonstration of typographic analysis in a rather humbler place than I may have seemed to suggest. The first is a fact which, in my view, made it all superfluous. There is, in line 19 of the *Oath*, a tiny speck of white on the 'M' of 'Moreover'. It was George Throckmorton, the Utah state documents examiner, who noticed that this was not due to a printing fault, nor yet to a defect in the printing surface. It was caused by a tiny chip of photographic emulsion which had attached itself to the negative used for the line block while in the process house; it was still there when the police discovered the negative. As proof that the cunning forgery of the *Oath* stemmed from this negative, this was incontrovertible. The other fact relates again to the border of the *Oath*. My own first suspicions were aroused not by any of the appearances I have tried to demonstrate, but the simple fact that the border was too close to the text. Having handled, and indeed dropped, formes myself, I could not see how the printers could have put so little furniture between the text and the border, and risked a pie with their make-shift equipment.

I will wind up very quickly by saying there are perhaps one or two moral lessons to be drawn from this. The first is that all the equipment in the world will not reveal a fake if you do not know what to look for. Secondly, if you think that Mr Hofmann is the last word, you are sadly mistaken. Owing to the increase in the price of artifacts of all sorts at the moment, with Van Gogh going up to £34 million, forgers are springing up everywhere. Somebody produced a Columbus letter, Texas is full of forged Declarations of the Independent State of Texas, and a man has just been put in prison for forging the complete text of the first printed Haggadah, Salamanca, *c.*1491–2. Lastly, greed, whether collectors' greed, booksellers' greed, or the altruistic greed of churches, is the manure on which forgery grows like mushrooms. Greed springs eternal in the human breast, but honesty is the best policy: *magna est veritas*, and let us hope that it will prevail.

Forged Handwriting

TOM DAVIS

TO STUDENTS of literature and history, Bibliography means primarily 'the study of books as material objects'.[1] If 'books' include manuscripts, then there is one aspect of the subject that fulfils that definition particularly well: the study of forgery. The difference between a forged and a genuine document will usually have absolutely nothing to do with content, and everything to do with form: one could say that in this sense the detection of forgery is the purest kind of bibliographical pursuit. This is rather anomalous, since those who actually pursue this pure bibliographical pursuit professionally are not in fact bibliographers at all, but forensic scientists; and between bibliographers and forensic scientists there seems to be a deep semantic chasm: normally, they are unaware of each other's existence.

I can offer my own experience as one of the few exceptions to this. Fortuitously, and fortunately, I have a foot in both camps. Since 1973 I have taught a three-year undergraduate course at Birmingham University called Bibliography and Paleography. This unique product of the imagination and energy of its founder, Peter Davison, is the only course on Bibliography that I know of that has both the space and time (12 students study the subject for two hours a week plus practical work, for three years) to deal with the subject both extensively and deeply. Secondly, since 1974 I have operated as what lawyers call a handwriting expert, and what document analysts call a document analyst: in other words, I give expert evidence in courts about all manner of forged, anonymous, and otherwise suspect documents. I operate part-time, of course, and do on average about three complete cases a month; I have given evidence in court many times, and have been involved with a remarkably wide range of human fallibility: my current case-load has 34 files in it (the law works exceedingly slowly ...), and includes cases concerning bigamy, blackmail, armed robbery (two), burglary, and the ownership of a rather expensive dog. As well as practising document analysis, I have also thought about it and taught it: the second year of the Bibliography course is devoted mostly to forensic matters, and I have been involved with rather a lot of research on the subject, some of which was funded by the Home Office in the form of large-scale projects.

Elsewhere I have written an informal and general introduction to the subject of document analysis for non-practitioners, and so have no need to do that again here.[2] What I propose to do in this paper is to discuss one aspect of my work, forgery, or, more strictly, the simulation of some aspects of the handwriting movement. I shall begin by defining the problem, and will do so by recounting two sample cases, which give some idea of the kind of real-life situations that provide the daily bread of document analysts. Having set out the problem, I shall attempt to answer it by opening up the subject of how forgery takes place: the mechanics of it, as it were, considered in a context of the mechanics of writing itself; what happens in the bones, muscles, and central nervous system when skilled cursive handwriting is produced. I shall emerge from this, I hope, with a theory of handwriting, and therefore a theory of forged handwriting, which I will then apply to my two real-life cases.

The cases

The first case I shall discuss is not at first sight forgery at all. I was telephoned urgently by a solicitor (this is rather normal) in a state of some agitation, and rushed in to examine a document actually in the middle of a trial. The first noticeable thing about the case was that as I went into Court I had to pass by a demonstration: a group of people holding up banners protesting the innocence of the client, several of which made odd references to plastic bags. These items do not normally play much part in document cases, but when I was shown the disputed signatures, the point of the reference became clear.

I was asked to examine two sets of what are known as Contemporaneous Notes. These are essentially transcripts of conversations between officers and the defendant, and are alleged to have been taken down by a police officer contemporaneously with the conversation. The defendant is invited to sign each page at least once, and, at the end of the document, to write in his or her own hand the 'caption': that is, a short formal statement agreeing that the transcript is authentic and faithful. The notes are then countersigned by two police officers, *even if the defendant has refused to sign them*, and are sometimes even the sole or principal evidence against a particular defendant. In these cases it is obviously open to the defendant to deny the accuracy of the record, in spite of the caption, or to allege that the whole document is a fabrication and that the signatures and captions are forged.[3]

In this case, however, the defendant's claim was not of forgery pure and simple, but of coercion. The first set of notes constituted the sample or comparison writing, and was not disputed. It bore a number of signatures of the defendant (who was, incidentally, charged with armed robbery) and the usual caption, all written in a not very sophisticated but clear and firm looped cursive hand. The second set of notes, which was made 24 hours later, was rather dramatically different. Unfortunately I am not able to illustrate this: cameras are not allowed in Court, and I must rely on words to describe the oddity of this writing. The notes bore signatures and caption, as usual, and both were in recognizably the same hand, but a dramatically different version of it: they exhibited a very evident tremor, such that most of the straight lines showed what amounted to a highly regular wave formation; but the curves of the waveforms were strangely well-formed, as if they had been written quickly and without hesitation.

The defence allegation was that the defendant had been forced to sign this second, disputed, document, against his will, since, he said, the entire conversation it contained was a fabrication from beginning to end. Hence the relevance of the plastic bags: if you put a plastic bag over someone's head, as the defence was alleging had happened, and threaten not to take it off until he signs a document, this might well act as a powerful persuader, but one that is very hard to prove; so what the defence wanted was for me to attest that the tremor in the handwriting was evidence for this particular method of coercion.

What I had to decide, in fact, was between two claims: either, as the defence would say, that the tremor was caused by this method of coercion, or, as the police would presumably allege, that the tremor was artificial: in other words, that it was forged. So although this is not immediately a forgery case as such, in fact, like most of the problems I examine, it came down to an allegation of forgery from one side or another.

The question that this case raises opens up a whole series of further questions: What causes tremor? Can it be forged successfully? What is it in the mechanisms of natural handwriting that allow this kind of deformity, whether under stress or from whatever cause? To answer these questions, the whole mechanism of handwriting needs to be examined.

The second case is less dramatic, and certainly much lower down in the hierarchy of crime, though it seemed to have caused no less suffering to the individuals concerned; it concerns the alleged theft of a consignment of denim jeans. Here is the story. There were two shops, unfortunately adjacent, each specializing in the sale of denim clothing of various kinds, mostly jeans, and both owned by Asian families. One of them was much bigger than the other. A lorry was despatched with two consignments of jeans, one for each store. A few days later, the smaller store phoned to say that their consignment had not arrived. The lorry driver produced two receipts, one for each consignment, both signed by Mohammed Anwar, the son of the proprietor of the larger store. But Anwar denied having received the jeans or signing two delivery notes. The police were called in (one suspects that not much love was lost between the two neighbouring stores) and eventually they brought a prosecution against Anwar for stealing the jeans.

My job was to examine the delivery notes. I reproduce them here, and invite the reader to contemplate them, together with a set of 'request samples' of Anwar's signature. The two delivery note signatures are beyond question different: the problem is, how to interpret the difference? One allegation would be that the second signature is a forgery of the first – presumably, if so, not exactly the work of a master of the forger's art – and the counter-allegation would be that the oddities of the second signature were the result of deliberate disguise on the part of Mr Anwar: in a sense that he was deliberately reproducing (forging, one might say) the signs of forgery.

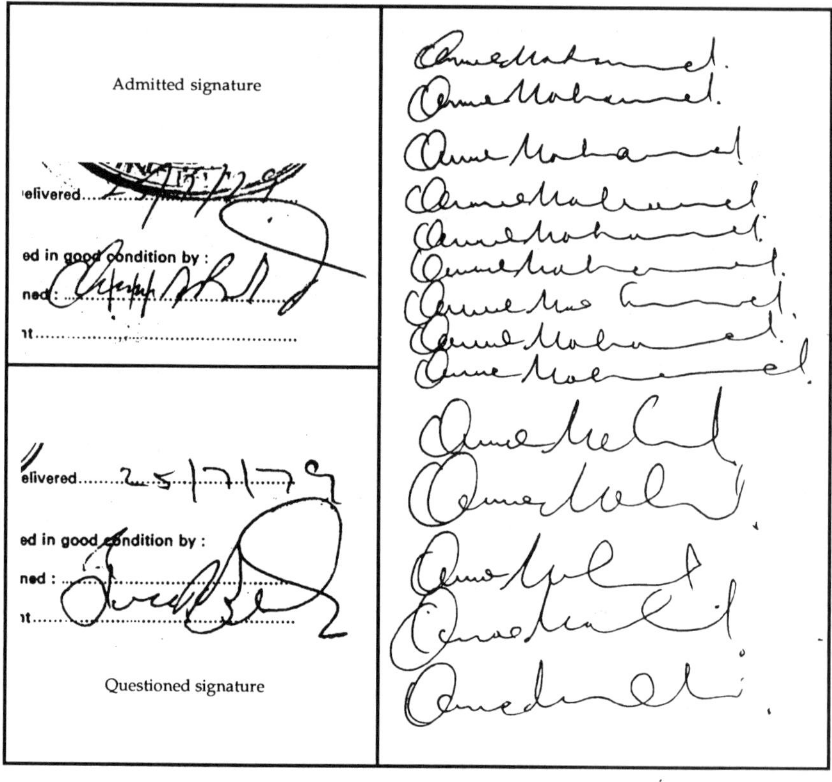

Questioned and sample signatures: Anwar Mohammed.

What, then, are these signs of forgery? What is it in the mechanisms of natural handwriting that do not show these signs, which are exhibited in the unnatural act of forgery? To answer authentic forgery? What is the difference between these questions, the whole mechanism of handwriting needs to be examined.

Line quality and rhythm

The key concept is what document examiners call '*line quality*', which seems to be the same as the paleographic concept '*ductus*', and has some relationship to the calligraphers' term 'movement'. Line quality refers to the degree of smoothness of the pen line. Good line quality is smooth, confident, with regular uninterrupted curves. Bad line quality is irregular; the curves are interrupted, tending to degenerate into a series of straight lines, showing pausing, or even *pen-lifts*, where the pen is taken completely off the paper. It is a matter of degree of skill, and speed. If our expertise in writing is inhibited in some way, the pen will move slowly, and the line quality will degenerate accordingly. In the act of forgery, since we are necessarily not as expert at producing the graphic shapes of someone else's writing as the writer will be, then the pen will move more slowly and the line quality of our imitation will be poorer than that of the original. Or so the theory goes, at any rate.

A related concept is 'rhythm': not a term used much by document analysts, but one that educationists and behavioural psychologists used to be fond of,[4] since it denotes (rather loosely) the combination of uniformity of speed and regularity of shape that characterizes what we find to be well-formed about skilled cursive handwriting. It reflects a feeling that until recently has been hard to define precisely, that a skilled writer works to a rhythm: that he or she takes the same amount of time to do similar component actions, with a resulting economy of movement and uniformity of shape.

These two terms certainly mean something, but their meaning is insufficiently precise, because it is untheorized. Those experienced in the field will know well what they mean, and certainly the term 'line quality' is used convincingly by document examiners in giving evidence. But recent work is not satisfied with the kind of experience-based assertion that was characteristic of an earlier generation of document examiners: it seeks to know the underlying causes of the phenomena it describes. In order to do this, it is necessary to understand the way in which handwriting works – the interaction of bone, muscle, and brain that produces skilled handwriting. This is what I now propose to outline. I find it useful to approach this rather difficult topic from both ends, as it were: from the physical structure of the hand and arm, which can then lead us into a possible model of the behavioural mechanisms that allow these physical components to operate successfully (or otherwise); and at the same time from the other end, attempting in a rather abstract way to model the process of handwriting, as if for instance we were attempting to teach a computer to write: if so, what would be the best kind of program to use? When we put the two together, we should have some kind of picture of what goes on in skilled handwriting.[5]

Bone structure and writing

We begin with the bones. Here, to save bulking the paper out with diagrams, I shall invite a certain amount of audience participation. Please, reader, hold up your hand, palm facing your face. Bend your fingers. You will immediately see what you have in fact always known, that the fingers themselves each consist of three bones, which are connected to each other by hinges: they can only open and close, and moreover only open until the finger is straight, but no further. (I assume in this and what follows that your anatomy is reasonably normal: there are those who can transcend the normal limitations to a surprising extent.) These bones (the *phalanges*, for those that like technical terms) join what we call the palm, which in a skeleton, rather unnervingly, does not exist: skeletons appear to have only very long fingers, that come straight from the complex of small bones (the *carpals*) that we call the wrist. The bones that join the wrist to the fingers (the *metacarpals*) have a ball-and-socket joint where they join the phalanges, and a similar, though looser, arrangement at the carpal end, but each of these joints is in fact very restricted: there is little we can do with the joints at the base of the fingers except open and shut (flex and extend, technically speaking) the fingers themselves. The thumb has a similar but much freer arrangement: we can wave the thumb about with a certain amount of abandon, which is why we can do all of the many interesting things that we do with our hands. The wrist, however, has only a very restrained flexibility: it can flex and extend the hand through perhaps 100°, but is capable of very little bending from side to side. Although it is a ball-and-socket joint, it behaves like a hinge.

Please now pick up a pen and hold it in the classic prescribed penhold. To do this (many people don't, for whatever reason) the side of the hand, that part stretching from the wrist to the base of the little finger, should rest on the paper. The thumb, forefinger, and second finger meet at their tips, surrounding the pen and holding it at about 2–3 cm. from its point. These fingers and the thumb should be flexed slightly but not too much; they should in fact be relaxed until they actually come to do any writing. The remaining two fingers are bent inwards somewhat and also rest supportively on the paper. The barrel of the pen rests on the fleshy web between forefinger and thumb. The hand is somewhat *pronated;* in other words, the forearm is rotated slightly to put pressure on the point of the pen, using principally the muscles of the upper arm and shoulder; this pronation is possible in spite of the fact that the elbow is a hinge, which cannot permit rotation, because the two bones of the forearm can cross each other to form an x-shape.

This, as I say, is the recommended penhold, and the way in which you were probably taught to write. Many people write differently, and as far as I know when they do so they are making some sort of satisfactory accommodation with their own particular musculature, mental set, and acculturation, and should continue to do so. Other penholds may well be equally efficient, and this one seems to be culturally specific, judging by illustrations of, for instance, medieval or classical scribes, and therefore optional. Though I would recommend that if during writing with an alternative penhold you notice that your knuckles are significantly white you should, as they say, consider your position.

Now, write. What happens? Firstly, the fingers flex and extend; on the whole, they do nothing more complicated than that. In other words, the hinges of the phalanges open and shut a little, which is all they can do. The fingers make no contibution to speak of to the sideways movement of the pen. This is effected by a series of accommodations: first the flexion (twisting backwards, one could call it) of the hand, pivoting at the hinge-like joint at the wrist, which is itself anchored to the paper at its lower edge. When the comfortable limits of this movement are reached, the fixed pivot at the wrist is moved over by a few centimetres, as the forearm pivots on a fixed point at the elbow, a movement which is permitted by, perhaps rather surprisingly, the capacity of the upper arm to rotate in the shoulder joint.

The fundamental movement of handwriting

If these observations of the basic components of skilled handwriting are correct, then it is clear that the way the bones relate to each other in the hand, arm, and shoulder collaborate to provide two distinct elements: an up-and-down and a sideways movement, producing some form of wave formation. This suggests that the basis for cursive handwriting is not in fact the joined production of individual letters, but modifications on a basic wave-form. In one way, this is counter-intuitive: we are accustomed, from looking at print and from the fact that we originally learned the letters in an unjoined print script, to think of them as discrete complex events, rather than syncopations of a basic wave; but in another way this feels (to me, at any rate) like an intuitively satisfying way of thinking about 'joined up' writing.

Confirmation comes from an odd source: graphologists tell us that all cursive handwriting is, at base, either arcaded, garlanded, or 'saw-tooth'. What this means is that if you write, as fast as you can, a series of /m/s (say), fast to the point of deforming the letters, then they will turn into an undifferentiated sequence of minims; these minims will either remain as /m/s, in which case your writing is said to be fundamentally arcaded; or it will turn into a sequence of /u/s, in which case your writing is garlanded; or it will turn out to be a zig-zag, in which case you are a 'saw-tooth' writer. We need not follow the graphologists into making deductions about the personality of the writer from these tendencies; what they say seems to be true enough at the physical level, and certainly supports our hypothesis about the wave-form base of cursive handwriting.

Rather more compelling support comes from attempts to produce computer models of the handwriting process.[6] The initial attempt involved the computer control of a mechanical arm, but the same principles apply if you simply wish to make a cursor produce a cursive handwriting-like trace by moving across a VDU screen: the question is, what is the smallest and most efficient set of instructions that you need to give the computer for it to be able to imitate handwriting? The first attempts involved coding for each of the letter-forms, and then writing a series of instructions that covered all of the possible varieties of joins that are necessary. This is very clumsy, involving a number of ad-hoc rules, which would need to be committed to the memory and addressed at need. This takes time, too much time; and it doesn't satisfy the intuitive feeling that handwriting is *rhythmic* – an activity whose basic pattern is regular in time; in other words, wave-like.

It was found, in fact, that if you program a basic wave form as the model of handwriting, and then instruct the computer with a relatively small set of cornering rules to account for what I have called the syncopations of the wave, you can describe the rules of handwriting rather economically. This doesn't of course prove that that is the way the brain itself does handwriting: brains are not computers, or even necessarily at all like them. But since we don't really know much about what brains *are* like, the computer sometimes, if used cautiously, can provide a useful metaphor; as, I would suggest, it does in this case.

A final confirmation of this theory comes from computer-assisted observation of the amount of time that people take to produce the elements of cursive handwriting. It has been shown that, quite precisely, the same amount of time is taken to make the short vertical strokes of an x-height minim, say in an /n/ or /u/ or /m/, as the longer verticals of an /l/ or an /h/.[7] Here clearly is a confirmation, and indeed the basis of a precise definition, of the concept of rhythm in handwriting, and a further support for the wave-form theory.

We can hypothesise, moreover, that skilled cursive handwriting is not done piecemeal, letter by letter, but in bursts: packages of information are sent down from the brain for realization by the muscles of the hand and arm. These may be a word, or even a small group of words in length. They consist of a set of coded instructions that provide the means of converting a fundamental wave-form into a handwritten set of (one hopes) legible letters.

This is easy to see in the case of the signature. When I am expounding this doctrine to my students, I ask them to do the following: to *draw* their signature, slowly, paying careful attention to the way it is formed. Usually more than half find this difficult, sometimes even impossible, to do: clearly for them the signature is resident in the memory as a pattern, and the brain sends down the command 'do signature' rather than, say, 'write "Tom Davis"'. Hence too the awkward phenomenon of 'forgetting one's signature', when a bank clerk asks you to do it again on the back of the cheque. A signature is an automatic process for most people; if it were not, we would not be able to do it so fast. And the same is true to a lesser extent for the handwriting skill in general. Skilled writers, which means most literate people, are not fully aware of just how difficult handwriting is: a very fine, delicate and quickly performed activity, perhaps the most dextrous thing that most of us do; but because we learned it so long ago and do it so well, it is routine and trivial for us. And it is only because of the automatic nature of so much of it that we are able to do it all. The difference between skilled movement and unskilled movement is that the former has been practised so many times that it needs very little intervention from the conscious mind: just the initiating instruction, really. The rest is left to the learned reflexes, and the mind can get on with the really difficult task of wondering what next to say.

Monitoring

There is however a crucial element missing from the model of handwriting that is now emerging, and that is a feedback or monitoring component. I have described a way of modelling what it is that we do, when we do handwriting; but when we send the set of coded instructions for the muscles to perform, how do we know that they are getting it right? The intuitive answer might be, we watch what we are doing; but this is not the answer. If, reader, you try writing with your eyes shut, you will probably find that you can do it surprisingly well; you will have problems about line length, naturally, and the essentially curved nature of the sideways movement (pivoting, as we have seen, around one moving and one fixed point), means that there may be trouble over keeping the base-line straight, but the detail of letter-formation is not hard to do blindfold. Obviously so, when you think about it: reaction time to a visual stimulus is relatively slow, because of the length of the feedback loop, from eye through the brain down to the hand, and the movement of the pen point on the paper is much faster than the eye can monitor efficiently.

There seem in fact to be two other kinds of monitoring going on. The first of these is known as *proprioceptive* feedback. This is that essential mechanism which enables us to know the position of any part of our body without having to look at something to orient it. So we can clap our hands with our eyes shut, because we seem to have a mental model of our body, that is continually updated by information from the very muscles that are themselves producing the movements that necessitate an update of the model. Not just clapping our hands, or, say, touching one forefinger tip to another quickly, something we may not be too confident of doing blindfold, but all of the things that the able-bodied are extremely good at, such as walking or standing up, for instance, depend vitally on proprioception. And particularly they depend upon the extreme rapidity with which the mental self-image is updated. Proprioception can do this because of the shortness of the feedback loop, which itself is a consequence of the fact that the muscles are, as the name suggests, self-observing: proprio-ceptive. They tell themselves what to do, without having to make the long trip up to the brain to do so. Because we privilege the eyes as a way of finding out about the world, partly I suppose for cultural reasons, we tend to ignore this extremely important mechansim; but if we did not have it, we would be as helpless as beached whales, out of our element.

It is the proprioceptive feedback mechanism that makes the difference between skilled and unskilled activity. If we don't know how to do something, we look, think, and then do – clumsily. If we are good at it, we just do, without thinking. The result is what the psychologist Luria nicely calls 'kinetic melody': smooth skilled action.[8] Whereas, reliance on the visual feedback mechanism results in pausing, as the visual information is processed and acted upon: the resulting action is jerky, irregular, and clumsy. At this point the reader may well see the practical application of this rather abstract discourse; forego, however, please, the delights of closure for a moment, because there is more to come.

This mechanism, I would conjecture, will tell the writer that he or she is doing the letters in more or less the correct way: when we feel the second upstroke of the /u/ is about to get too long, proprioception, quicker than thought, warns us to stop. This explains too why if we are cold, or old, or ill, or drunk, the handwriting may either increase or decrease, consistently or inconsistently, in size: all of these states can cause a general slowing down in the flow of information round the central nervous system, and so we may receive the message to go into reverse at the end of the second upstroke of the /u/, but take a little longer to go about obeying it; thus the size of the letters increases. Or, alternatively, we may be aware of our slower-than-normal state, and put an instruction into the system to compensate for it; if we overcompensate, then the handwriting becomes smaller.

This explanation is satisfactory, up to a point; but some psychologists of skilled behaviour go further, and suppose the existence of another kind of monitoring procedure that is even finer and faster in its effects.[9] Whether this is a separate mechanism, in fact, or just another aspect of the proprioceptive system, is disputed; but for our purposes it is certainly helpful to distinguish the two.

Whereas the first mechanism tells the body when to stop doing what it is doing and do something else, this mechanism is what enables it to *go on* doing what it is doing when it doesn't want to do anything else. It monitors the state of rest or motion of some part of the model of the body, and warns us when that desired state of rest or motion is in danger of ceasing – or, rather, when the state is in danger of moving beyond some tolerance that we have decided (unconsciously) upon: perfect rest or motion does not happen in nature.

A useful and economical way of doing that is by using a system analogous with the mechanism in a thermostat. Here the monitor is constantly aware of temperature. When it senses that the temperature has gone below a set level, it tells the heater to come on. There is a pause, while the room heats up, and then the thermostat will notice that the room is too hot and turn the heater off. This is an economical way of doing the job; the mechanism is simple, and the results can be as quick as one needs them to be. But they can never be quick enough to maintain absolute adherence to the set temperature: however finely tuned the relationship between the heater and the monitor, the temperature will fluctuate, regularly; if we can graph this fluctuation with a precision appropriate to the degree of variation, this graph will form a wave.

In handwriting the pen traces its own record of the movement of the hand that controls it. It is normally not a fine enough trace to record the fluctuations of this autocompensatory monitoring mechanism; until, that is, this starts to act inefficiently. When it does, we see what we call tremor in the handwriting: a rather regular flunctuation in what should be a straight line or a smooth curve. This differs from impairment of the proprioceptive function, which characteristically results in poor line quality based on slowness of the pen movement; tremor is normally rather fast, and it is possible to produce handwriting with marked tremor but good line quality.

Our theoretical model is now complete: we have the means of explaining the phenomena of handwriting in which we are interested. In brief: the defects in line quality associated with forgery are caused by using the visual rather than the proprioceptive feedback mechanism; while the tremor that can be caused by stress can be related to the autocompensatory servomechanism.

The cases, again

We can now return to the two handwriting problems and see how our model can be applied. In the case of the allegedly plastic-bag-induced signatures, we have the finest example of tremor that I have ever seen, absolutely pure, and free from any infection from poor line quality. My normal experience of tremor is in the handwriting of old people, where, because of the multi-causal nature of the symptoms associated with impairment in old age, there is usually a large variety of other handwriting phenomena accompanying tremor. The client in this case was rather fit, and his handwriting therefore reinforces my theoretical model rather well.

For him, however, the more important question was, does it show that he was coerced? I gave evidence in this case, and pointed out firstly that clearly something fairly spectacular had happened to his handwriting in the 24 hours between both sets of samples; secondly, that little is known about the specific effects of stress on handwriting, because the Social Science Research Council rather frowns on the torture of experimental subjects[10]; thirdly, however, his symptoms were consistent with the results of, among other things, old age, drugs, alcohol, having just run round the block, or, indeed, stress. The Court, perhaps reflecting that the other items in the list were probably not relevant, supported his appeal on the charge; to what extent their decision was based on my evidence, I do not know.

With regard to Mohammed Anwar, here, it seems to me, we have a gross and obvious case of forgery. Anwar's own handwriting shows rather well a predominance, if anything, of the rhythmic wave-form, resulting in a certain careless disregard for the number of minims in any given signature, as can be seen in the request samples. For the curious, who may perhaps find the other admitted receipt signature a little difficult to read, I can say that Anwar, under close questioning from me, explained that it consisted of the words 'Anwar Mohd', the latter being a normal abbreviation of 'Mohammed'. He was unable to explain consistently which pen-strokes produced which letter, however: a very clear example of the signature being written as a pattern, rather than a string of letters, shown here rather starkly because it is obvious that the pattern got itself scrambled in the transmission.[11]

What of the questioned signature? Well, in my opinion this is a forgery, as I said. It shows very well, because it is so very bad, the defects of forgery: proprioception is replaced by visual input and monitoring, and the result is poor line quality, pausing, pen lifts – defects galore, one might say: the very reverse of Anwar's normal practice. Could Anwar have been disguising his own signature – forging a forgery? I very much doubt it. One's signature is so ingrained, particularly in a writer like Anwar, that it is hard to forget so totally and entirely how to do it; some at least of that basic pattern would surely come through. And to do so in the few minutes (at most) between signing for one consignment of jeans and signing for another, having instantly formulated this really rather Machiavellian scheme, stretches credibility. In any case, there is another factor. It is quite clear to me that whoever produced the questioned signature was (a) imitating the admitted receipt signature, and (b) couldn't read it. He or she clearly thought that Anwar Mohammed had a capital /B/ somewhere in his name. For Anwar himself successfully to imitate inability to read his own signature, or even to think of such a thing, would be truly amazing.

The finger of suspicion seems to me to point rather squarely at the lorry-driver. I did not say so in Court, because the Defence advised me not to; they were aware of all the details of the case, as I was not, and in any case spectacular counter-accusations only happen in films. Anwar Mohammed's trial resulted in a hung jury; he was retried, found guilty, and fined a very substantial sum of money. The value of the jeans, the immediate cause of the two lengthy and painful trials, was about £200.00. I do not know why he was found guilty; one of the more frustrating aspects of being a document examiner is that, usually, and in some ways, blessedly, all that you see is the documents. The rest of the case, the complex and often agonizing interactions of human beings that constitute it, and indeed the real truth of the matter, are, normally, a closed book.

References

1. Philip Gaskell, *A New Introduction to Bibliography,* Oxford, 1972, p.1.
2. 'Forensic Handwriting Analysis', in *Talking About Text: Studies Presented to David Brazil*, English Language Research, Birmingham, 1986.
3. I should say here than in fourteen years, during which I have seen very many sets of Contemporaneous Notes, and in fact disputed confessions of all kinds, this present case apart, I have only ever seen one that I could demonstrate to have been fabricated.
4. See for instance F.N. Freeman, 'Experimental Analysis of the Writing Movement', *Yale Psychological Studies,* New Series II, i (1914), 7, and citations.

5. I should make it clear for the benefit of any psychologist of skilled behaviour who may read this that what follows is informal, and therefore incomplete; I will avoid as far as possible specialist vocabulary and highly technical description.

6. Described by John Hollerbach in 'A Competence Model for Handwriting', *Visible Language,* XIII, iii (1989), 252– 264. His work has been replicated and developed by Alan Wing at the MRC Applied Psychology, Cambridge.

7. See Alan Wing, 'Variability in Handwritten Characters', *Visible Language*, XIII, iii (1979), 283–298.

8. A.R. Luria, *The Working Brain*, translated by Basil Haigh, Penguin (1973), 31.

9. There is a good account of this in David Legge and Paul J. Barber, *Information and Skill*, Methuen, 1976, pp.67–70.

10. However: I had a brainwave while escorting my children round Alton Towers Amusement Park, and this eventually resulted in some interesting research conducted by my student Frances Brill, on the comparison of handwriting done before and after a trip on their vicious and terrifying roller-coaster ride. It is now being written up for publication.

11. The questioning took place while we were waiting to give evidence, and the straight lines that cut into the admitted delivery note signature are his attempt to show me where the different letters of his name are represented in it.

Index

[Numbers in *italics* refer to illustations]